SMART GUIDE

W9-DDW-287

CRE▲TIVE
HOMEOWNER®

wiring
step-by-step

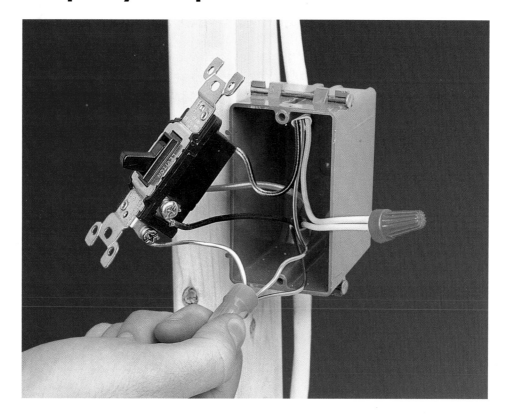

CREATIVE HOMEOWNER®, Upper Saddle River, New Jersey

SMART GUIDE: WIRING

MANAGING EDITOR	Fran J. Donegan
JUNIOR EDITOR	Jennifer Calvert
TECHNICAL EDITOR	Steve Willson
PHOTO COORDINATOR	Mary Dolan
TECHNICAL ADVISOR	Peter Eng
INDEXER	Schroeder Indexing Services
DIGITAL IMAGING SPECIALIST	Frank Dyer
SMART GUIDE® SERIES COVER DESIGN	Clarke Barre
FRONT COVER PHOTOGRAPHY	Brian C. Nieves/CH

CREATIVE HOMEOWNER

VICE PRESIDENT AND PUBLISHER	Timothy O. Bakke
MANAGING EDITOR	Fran J. Donegan
ART DIRECTOR	David Geer
PRODUCTION COORDINATOR	Sara M. Markowitz

Current Printing (last digit)
10 9 8 7 6 5 4 3 2 1

Manufactured in the United States of America

Smart Guide: Wiring, Second Edition
Library of Congress Control Number: 2009920819
ISBN-10: 1-58011-460-1
ISBN-13: 978-1-58011-460-8

CREATIVE HOMEOWNER®
A Division of Federal Marketing Corp.
24 Park Way
Upper Saddle River, NJ 07458
www.creativehomeowner.com

Photo Credits

All photography by Brian C. Nieves/CH, except as noted.

page 16: *left* John Parsekian/CH
page 26: *bottom right* John Parsekian/CH
page 40: *top right* Freeze Frame Studio/CH; *bottom left & right* Merle Henkenius
pages 46–47: *all* Freeze Frame Studio/CH
pages 86–87: *all* Merle Henkenius
page 108: *left* courtesy of Malibu Lighting/Intermatic, Inc.

Planet Friendly Publishing
✓ Made in the United States
✓ Printed on Recycled Paper
 Text: 10%   Cover: 10%
Learn more: www.greenedition.org

GREEN EDITION

contents

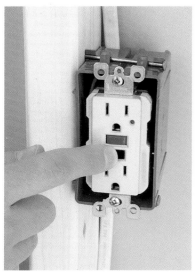

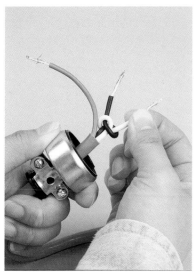

safety first

Though all the designs and methods in this book have been reviewed for safety, it is not possible to overstate the importance of using the safest construction methods possible. What follows are reminders; some do's and don'ts of do-it-yourself and electrical work. They are not substitutes for your own common sense.

- Always use caution, care, and good judgment when following the procedures described in this book.

- Always be sure that the electrical setup is safe; be sure that no circuit is overloaded, and that all power tools and electrical outlets are properly grounded. Do not use power tools in wet locations.

- Never modify a plug by bending or removing prongs. When prongs are bent, loose or missing, replace the entire device.

- Don't use 3-prong-to-2-prong cord adapters to overcome ground connections.

- Be sure all receptacles and electrical conductors are properly grounded.

- If a plug prong breaks off in a receptacle, do not attempt to remove it. Turn off the circuit, and call a licensed electrician.

- Be sure receptacles are mounted securely in their boxes and do not move when the plug is inserted. A loose receptacle can cause a short circuit.

- Do not use loose receptacles or other faulty electrical equipment until it is repaired or replaced and inspected by a licensed electrician.

- Replace all damaged electrical enclosures such as receptacle, switch, and junction boxes.

- Use extension cords only when necessary, on a short-term basis; never use extension cords in place of permanent wiring.

- Be sure all extension cords are properly sized and rated for the use intended.

- Keep electrical cords away from areas where they may be stepped on, pinched between door jambs, or otherwise damaged.

- Don't use appliance or extension cords that show signs of wear, such as frayed or dried sheathing or exposed wires.

- Visually inspect all electrical equipment and appliances before use.

- Never staple, nail, or otherwise attach an extension cord to any surface.

- Always turn off tools and appliances before unplugging them.

- Never unplug a tool or appliance by yanking on the cord; always remove the cord by the plug.

- Always keep the area in front of your main panel clear and dry. Work on a rubber mat or dry board and maintain an unobstructed area of at least 3 feet in front of the panel. The panel must be easily accessed.

- Keep dust, lint, and other combustible materials away from electrical panels, receptacles, and appliances.

- Keep electrical panel doors closed and latched when not in use.

- Keep all electrical equipment away from any source of water unless it is rated for use in wet areas, such as a wet-dry shop vacuum.

- Use ground-fault circuit interrupters (GFCIs) wherever possible. GFCIs are required in all wet, damp, or moist areas.

- Limit use of receptacles to one appliance. If more than one appliance will be on a circuit, use an approved plug strip with a built-in circuit breaker.

- Use proper lighting in areas where the risk of an electrical hazard is present and keep emergency backup lighting readily available.

- Keep all energized parts of electrical circuits and equipment enclosed in approved cabinets and enclosures.

- Use only tools that have double insulated casings.

- Always be aware of the potential hazards when doing electrical work of any kind.

- Be sure to use appropriate protective equipment when doing electrical work (safety glasses, insulated gloves, rubber mats, etc.).

introduction

WORKING EFFICIENTLY AND SAFELY with electricity requires an adequate knowledge of how electricity works. This knowledge often seems beyond the reach of the average homeowner, obscured by a veil of confusing codes, complicated formulas, and hieroglyphic symbols. To make matters worse, many supposedly basic books assume that you already have a working knowledge of electricity and electrical codes. *Smart Guide: Wiring* is designed to provide you with a basic understanding of how electricity works, how it is supplied to your home, and how you can work with it safely. It explains which wires to use, where they go, and what they do, as well as which tools and materials you will need to perform the work at hand.

Smart Guide: Wiring will teach you to approach your home wiring projects with the confidence that comes from knowledge. You will see that there is really nothing mystical about installing a dimmer switch or changing a receptacle. Like changing a lightbulb, the work can be simple once you know how to do it, and to do it safely.

As a teaching tool, *Smart Guide: Wiring* provides clear instruction, ease of use, and an entertaining presentation as its main attributes. Following are some of the features that help the book meet those criteria:

■ **Step-by-step photographs** illustrate how to wire electrical boxes, switches, receptacles, and even specific appliances. Great effort has been made to include photos that will help you to understand how circuits work, show you real components and wiring, and take you step-by-step through the installation and repair projects.

■ **Charts and tables** provide information, such as the correct size and type of wire for a particular project.

■ **Detailed how-to wiring diagrams** reinforce the step-by-step procedures and often add variations and alternative approaches.

■ **Pro Tips** provide tidbits of interesting and insightful information about various subjects.

Code Changes

The 2008–2011 National Electrical Code® contains changes that apply to new construction, additions, and alterations. They do not apply to repairs and the replacement of existing devices, but check with your local building department for exact requirements. Highlights include

Tamper-Proof Receptacles. All 125-volt, 15- and 20-ampere receptacles installed in living ares must be listed as tamper-proof. These receptacles are designed to prevent a child from inserting an object into the receptacle. (See page 63.)

Arc-Fault Circuit Interrupters. The previous code required this protection in circuits serving bedrooms. The protection is extended to all habitable living areas. (See page 27.)

GFCI Exceptions. The exceptions for GFCI receptacles in wet locations are deleted. They are now required on appliance-dedicated receptacles. (See page 68.)

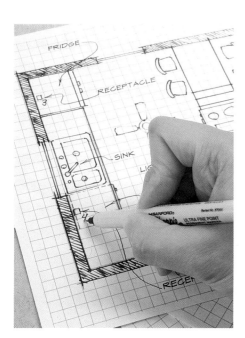
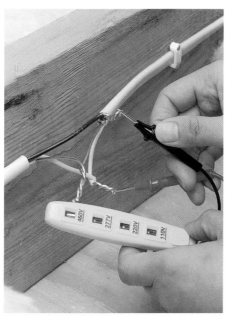
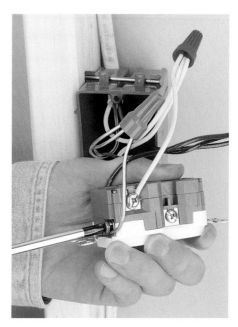

chapter 1

wiring basics

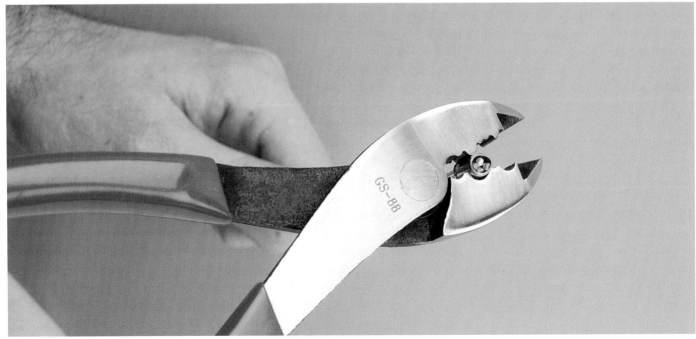

POSSESSING A BASIC KNOWLEDGE of electricity may not seem essential to doing electrical work, especially if you are using a "how-to" book with simple step-by-step instructions. However, nothing could be farther from the truth. Not every step in a process may be obvious, and very often knowing the basic theory behind a practice may enable you to figure out how to do something you have never done before. The purpose of this chapter is to give you a basic understanding of electricity—what it is, how it is provided, how it works, and how you can work with it safely.

Fundamentals of Electricity

Electricity Defined

Electricity is nothing more than an organized flow of electrons and protons behaving in response to the attraction of oppositely charged particles and the repulsion of like-charged particles. If you can get enough electrons to break free of their orbits and start flowing in one direction or another, you have a flow of current. This current, or power, is defined as electricity. The device that frees the electrons from their orbit is called a power generator. To create vast amounts of electrical power, large generators, such as those operated by utility companies, must be turned on a massive scale.

Terminology of Electricity

As with most subjects, electricity has its own vocabulary. For this book, however, it is important to know the meaning of only four key terms: ampere (amperage), volt (volt-age), watt (wattage), and ohms (resistance). By mastering these terms, you will better understand electricity.

Ampere: An *ampere,* or *amp,* measures the rate, or quantity, of electrical flow. A typical contemporary home, for example, might have an electrical system of 150 to 200 amps. Amperage, in contrast, is the actual measure of current flowing in a circuit to an appliance. Although this can be measured only when the circuit is turned on, the rating of an electric appliance, in volts and amperes, or volts and watts, is required by the National Electrical Code (Section 422.60) to be marked on the identifying nameplate of the appliance. Amperes are designated by the letter A.

Ampacity is the amount of current in amperes a wire can safely conduct. Determining the correct ampacity of a wire is important because using an incorrect-size wire can create a fire hazard. Each wire carries a limited amount of current before it will heat to the point of damaging its insulation. For example, a 14-gauge wire can take a maximum current of 15 amps, a 12-gauge wire 20 amps, and so on. If a wire is too small for a job, generated heat can destroy its insulation, causing a fire. Amperage ratings are also important when you buy fuses or circuit breakers. Amperage of fuses or breakers, circuits, and appliances must match. Too little fuse or circuit-breaker amperage will cause these protection devices to blow or trip. Too much will permit a dangerous amount of overcurrent, or flow, which occurs when too many appliances are used on the same circuit or during a power surge. The result is overheating of the circuit, which will create a potential for fire.

Current Flow

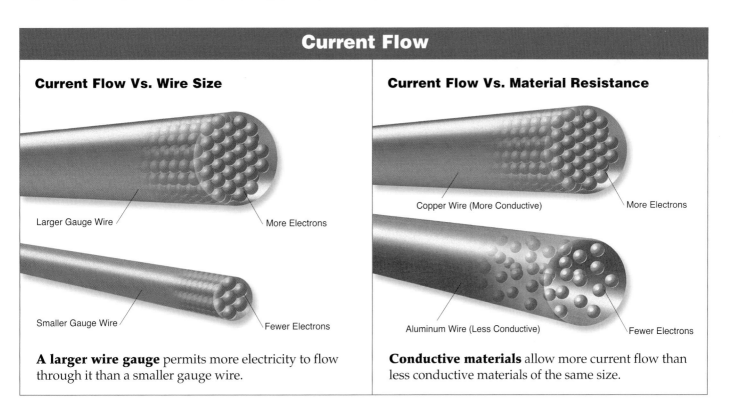

Current Flow Vs. Wire Size

Larger Gauge Wire — More Electrons

Smaller Gauge Wire — Fewer Electrons

A larger wire gauge permits more electricity to flow through it than a smaller gauge wire.

Current Flow Vs. Material Resistance

Copper Wire (More Conductive) — More Electrons

Aluminum Wire (Less Conductive) — Fewer Electrons

Conductive materials allow more current flow than less conductive materials of the same size.

Volt: A *volt* measures the pressure exerted by electrical power. *Voltage* is the moving (electromotive) force that causes current to flow in an electrical circuit. A generator creates the pressure that keeps the electrical current flowing through conductors, known as wires.

Voltage, designated by the letter V, pushes a current that alternates between positive and negative values. This is known as an *alternating current* (AC). It periodically reverses, or alternates, direction in cycles, called *Hertz.* One cycle takes 1/60 second to complete. This is usually expressed as a rate of 60 cycles per second. The average voltage on this cycle is measured at 120 volts on the return, or neutral, wire and 240 volts across both of the two hot utility wires entering a home.

Contemporary three-wire residential wiring carries both 120- and 240-volt power. Large appliances like air conditioners, electric ranges, and clothes dryers typically use 240-volt wiring. Electrical devices must be labeled with their operating voltage level. This means that the product has been designed to operate at the listed voltage only. Do not, for example, hook up an electrical device rated at 125 volts to a circuit that supplies 220 to 240 volts. You'll burn it out.

Watt, Wattage: In practical terms, *wattage* is the amount of energy used to run a particular appliance. The wattage rating of a circuit is the amount of power the circuit can deliver safely, which is determined by the current-carrying capacity of the wires or cables. Wattage also indicates the amount of power a fixture or appliance needs to work properly.

To calculate the wattage, or *power,* available in a circuit, first determine its amperage (amp rating). It will be marked on the circuit breaker or fuse for that circuit in the service-entrance, or main, panel— 15 or 20 amps for most room cir-

American Wire Gauges

Wire Diameter (Gauge)		Ampacity (Current Capacity)	Volts (Power Capacity)	Typical Usage
	18	7 Amps	**24 Volts** (134 Watts) Continuous load	**Low-Voltage Wiring** Bells, chimes, timers, thermostats, etc.
	16	10 Amps	**24 Volts** (192 Watts) Continuous load	**Light-Duty Wiring** Low-voltage lighting, etc.
	14	15 Amps	**120 Volts** (1,440 Watts) Continuous load	**Common House Wiring** Receptacles, lights, some A/Cs
	12	20 Amps	**120 Volts** (1,920 Watts) **240 Volts** (3,840 Watts) Continuous load	**Common House Wiring** Receptacles, lights, small appliances
	10	30 Amps	**120 Volts** (2,880 Watts) **240 Volts** (5,760 Watts) Continuous load	**Large Appliances** Clothes dryers, room A/Cs
	8	40 Amps	**240 Volts** (7,680 Watts) Continuous load	**Large Appliances** Central A/Cs, electric ranges
	6	55 Amps	**240 Volts** (10,560 Watts) Continuous load	**Large Appliances** Central A/Cs, electric ranges, furnaces

The NEC requires that all conductors and cables be marked to indicate their AWG size, at intervals not to exceed 24 inches (Section 310.11). Each wire size can carry a limited amount of current under continuous load (80 percent of its maximum), which is defined as operating for 3 hours or more. The measure of how much current a wire can safely conduct is called its ampacity.

cuits, 30 to 50 amps for most heavy-duty circuits. Then, **Watts = Volts x Amps.** A 15-amp circuit with 120 volts carries 1,800 watts (15 x 120); a 20-amp circuit carries 2,400 watts (but not under continuous load).

Resistance: Electrical *resistance,* measured in *ohms,* restricts the flow of current. The higher the resistance, the lower the current. This resistance causes a change of electrical energy into some other form of energy, usually heat. It is this heat, for example, that is used to warm the water in your water heater.

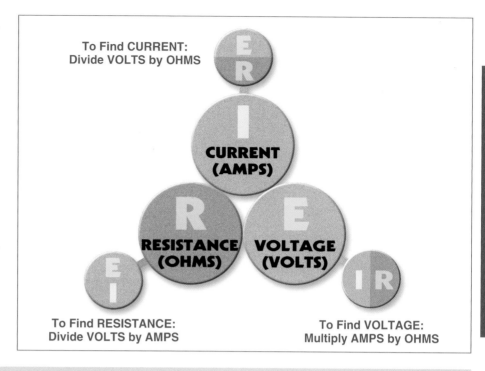

To Find CURRENT:
Divide VOLTS by OHMS

CURRENT
(AMPS)

RESISTANCE
(OHMS)

VOLTAGE
(VOLTS)

To Find RESISTANCE:
Divide VOLTS by AMPS

To Find VOLTAGE:
Multiply AMPS by OHMS

Calculating the Ampacity of an Electric Water Heater

If you want to install a new electric water heater in your home, you must first determine its capacity. Let's assume that you have a family of four in a home with two tubs/showers, one dishwasher, and one clothes washer. Referring to the table at right, "Usage Points," this gives you a total of 8 points. An adequately sized water heater for your home would have a 65-gallon capacity. A standard 65-gallon water heater has heating elements rated at 4,500 watts and 240-volt AC wiring. From this information, you can calculate how much current the water heater will use so that you can determine the correct-size wire to use when you install the heater. Because power (wattage) equals voltage (volts) multiplied by current (amps), and you know power and voltage, you can calculate the current:

**4,500 watts divided by 240 volts
equals 18.75 amps**

The wire-gauge table on page 8 indicates that a 12-gauge wire would be adequate to carry 20 amps. However, NEC Section 422.13 requires that the wires supplying the water heater have a capacity of 125 percent of the appliance (1.25 x 18.75A = 23.4 amperes). The wire-gauge table shows that the maximum continuous safe carrying capacity for a 12-gauge wire at 240 volts is 20 amps. The water heater exceeds this, so you must use the next-larger-size wire, which is a 10-gauge wire having an ampacity of 30 amps.

Usage Points

If your usage points equal	Then you need a
4 or less	40-gal. water heater
5 or 6	50-gal. water heater
7 or 8	65-gal. water heater
9 or more	80-gal. water heater

To select the proper size electric water heater for your home, calculate one usage point for each person, bathtub/shower, dishwasher, and clothes washer in your household, and consult the table to determine the capacity water heater that you need.

PRO TIP

Calculating Current

A quick way of calculating 240-volt current is to figure 4 amps per 1,000 watts of power (8 amps for 120-volt). In this water-heater example, you would divide 4,500 watts by 1,000, getting 4.5. Multiplying this by 4 amps yields 18 amps, which is close to the formula answer.

Appliance Ratings

Today, major appliances like freezers, refrigerators, and water heaters are energy-rated for the amount of power (wattage) they use. This information appears on a large yellow "Energy Guide Label" affixed to each device. Smaller appliances may not be so labeled, but their wattage rating should be listed on their packaging. The wattage rating can be used to calculate the actual operating cost of the appliance. The higher the wattage rating of the appliance, the more you will have to pay to operate it. For example, if a 4-foot-long baseboard heater uses 250 watts per foot, it will require 1,000 watts to run. At 10¢ per kilo-watt-hour (1,000 watts used by an appliance in one hour), it will cost 10¢ per hour to run the heater. If the wattage is not listed on the appliance, look for the voltage and current. Multiply the the two together to find the wattage.

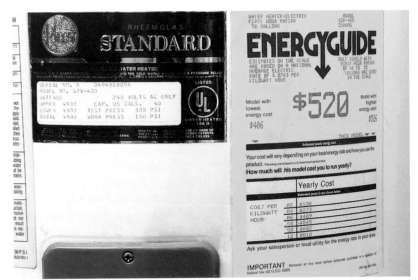

The energy-rating sticker on the side of this 4,500-watt water heater tells the prospective buyer approximately what he or she will be paying per year for the use of the appliance. Running a 4,500-watt water heater for one hour, at 10¢ per kilowatt-hour, would cost 4.5 x 10¢, or 45¢ per hour.

Appliance Wattage

Appliance	Average Wattage		
		Food mixer	150–250
		Frost-free refrigerator	400–600
		Frying pan	1,000–1,200
		Gas furnace	800
Attic fan	400	Garbage disposal	500–900
Blender	400–1,000	Hair dryer	400–1,500
Broiler	1,400–1,500	Hot plate	600–1,000
Can opener	150	Iron	600–1,200
Central air conditioner	2,500–6,000	Laser printer	1,000
Clock	2–3	Microwave oven	1,000–1,500
Clothes dryer	4,000–5,600	Oil furnace	600–1,200
Clothes washer	500–1,000	Portable heater	1,000–1,500
Computer with monitor	565	Radio	40–150
Coffee maker	600–1,500	Range	4,000–8,000
Crock pot	200–275	Range oven	3,500–5,000
Deep fat fryer	1,200–1,600	Refrigerator	150–300
Dehumidifier	500	Roaster	1,200–1,650
Dishwasher	1,000–1,500	Room air conditioner	800–2,500
Electric blanket	150–500	Sewing machine	60–90
Electric water heater	2,000–5,500	Stereo/CD player	50–140
Exhaust fan	75–200	Television	50–450
Floor polisher	300	Toaster oven	500–1,450
Food freezer	300–600	Waffle iron	600–1,200

Today, appliances are typically rated for how much power (wattage) that they draw. Because your utility bill states how much you pay per kilowatt-hour of electricity, this information can be used to calculate the actual operating cost of any appliance.

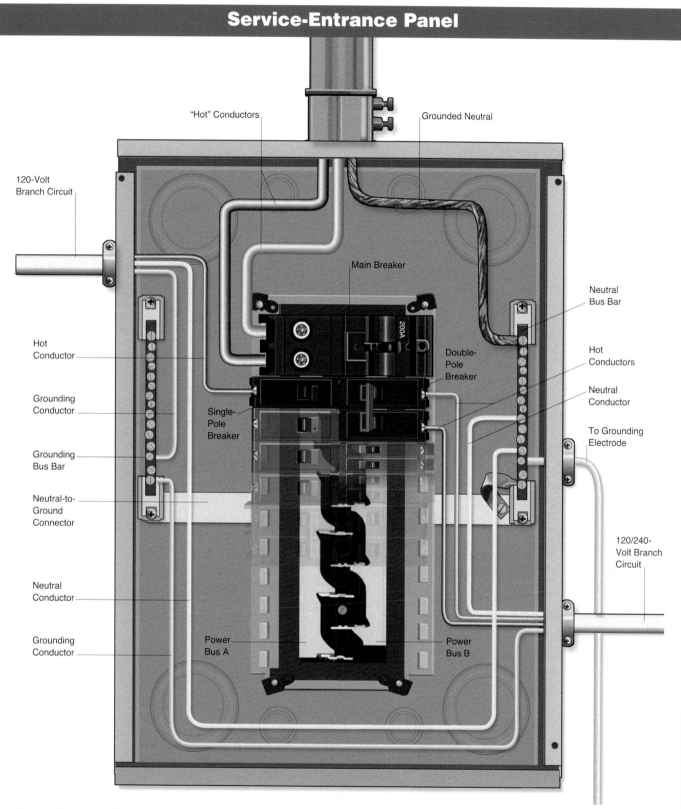

"Hot" Conductors

Grounded Neutral

120-Volt
Branch Circuit

Main Breaker

Neutral
Bus Bar

Hot
Conductor

200A

Double-
Pole
Breaker

Hot
Conductors

Grounding
Conductor

Neutral
Conductor

Single-
Pole
Breaker

To Grounding
Electrode

Grounding
Bus Bar

Neutral-to-
Ground
Connector

120/240-
Volt Branch
Circuit

Neutral
Conductor

Grounding
Conductor

Power
Bus A

Power
Bus B

Also called the circuit-breaker panel, the main service-entrance panel (SEP) is the distribution center for the electricity you use in your home. Incoming red and black hot wires connect to the main breaker and energize the other circuit breakers that are snapped into place. Hot (black or red) wires connected to the various circuit breakers carry electricity to appliances, fixtures, and receptacles throughout the house. White and bare-copper wires connect to the neutral and grounding bus bars, respectively. (Representative 120-volt and 120/240-volt circuits are shown.)

Working Safely with Electricity

Basic Rules of Safety

Safety is, without question, the most important aspect of any electrical work. One split-second mistake can result in serious injury or even death. Many errors are made because of impatience, ignorance, or unnecessary risk-taking. If you consider the potential cost of not following simple, common-sense rules of safety when you are working with electricity, then you will certainly realize the importance of avoiding such mistakes.

The first rule of working with electricity is to shut off the power at your main service-entrance panel before working on a circuit. Always keep a well-maintained flashlight near the panel so that when power is cut off you will not be left standing in the dark. Also, be sure to stand on a rubber mat or dry boards, especially if your utility room is damp, and use only one hand to remove or replace a fuse or flip a circuit-breaker switch. After shutting off the power, secure the panel so that no one else will accidentally turn the circuit back on while you are working on it. All circuits should be clearly marked to avoid confusion as to which circuit to shut off. Nevertheless, whenever you do work on a circuit, be doubly sure that it is not hot by testing it, using a circuit tester.

Second, be absolutely positive that you have carefully planned your work, that you know every step you'll take, and that you are not in over your head. For this reason, it is probably best to limit yourself to doing work outside your electrical panel. Leave adding circuits and making panel repairs to a licensed electrician.

Keep a well-maintained flashlight near your service-entrance panel, and always stand on a rubber mat or dry boards when working on the panel.

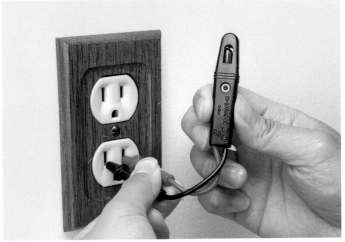

Before working on any circuit, test it to be sure that the power has been turned off. Test both receptacles on an outlet. It may be a split circuit.

To prevent a ladder from slipping out from under you when working outside, swivel the feet into a vertical position; then dig them into the ground.

Third, when doing actual wiring and electrical repairs, take precautions to use the correct tools, equipment, and techniques. For example, use a wooden or fiberglass ladder, never one that is made of metal; always wear safety glasses to protect yourself against sparks and flying debris; and make sure that all of your tools are properly insulated for electrical work. Be conscious of details, such as properly wrapping wire terminals with electrical tape and using the correct-size electrical boxes for the work you are doing. And, especially if you are working with power equipment outside, be certain that the electrical circuit is thoroughly protected by a ground-fault circuit interrupter (GFCI), or use a GFCI extension cord. (See bottom right.) If a tool malfunctions and has a fault to ground, this type of protection can save your life. For portable power tools, be sure to use heavy-duty 12-gauge extension cords. Undersized cords are a potential fire hazard. In addition, all electrical supplies should be UL-listed—which means that they carry the symbol of the Underwriters Laboratories, your assurance that the product meets the minimum safety standards set by this and other governing agencies.

Lastly, observe the rules and regulations established by your local, state or regional, building and electrical codes. Some codes may prohibit you from doing certain types of electrical work or using a particular type of electrical cable. Most local requirements are based on the National Electrical Code.

Short Circuits

When an accidental connection is made between two hot wires or one hot wire and a grounded wire, and excess current flows across the connection, this is known as a short circuit. A short-circuited device can be life-threatening if you come into physical contact with it. Because electrical current travels along the path of least resistance, you can literally become part of the electric circuit—the part through which the current attempts to flow back to its original source. Normally, this is done through a neutral wire in the circuit. However, for safety's sake, an alternative low-resistance route is usually provided by a green or bare grounding wire leading back to the panel box. The short causes the circuit breaker to shut off.

The grounding circuit typically connects all of the electrical devices, including fixtures, switches, receptacles, electrical boxes, and so on, to a terminal, or bus bar, in the main panel. The bus bar is in turn connected to a metal cold-water pipe and two grounding rods driven into the earth "such that at least 8 feet of length is in contact with the soil" [NEC Section 250.53(G)]. As an added precaution, individual appliances or tools that are metal-clad are connected to this grounding system through the third prong on a three-prong plug.

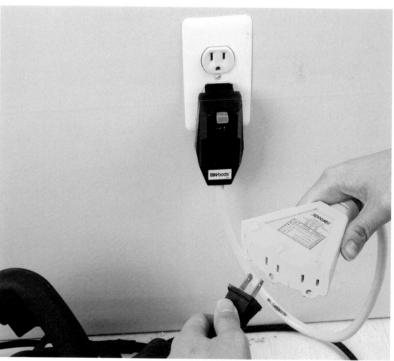

Always wear comfortable, adjustable safety glasses when doing electrical work, to protect yourself from flying debris or sparking wires.

AC power tools carry enough electrical current to cause electrocution. To be safe, use a heavy-duty extension cord that has a GFCI built directly into it.

Tools

Electrical projects require several specialized tools. They also require several standard hand and power tools, such as hammers, chisels, squares, and portable electric drills. You may already have many of these tools. However, if you do not, you may purchase or rent them on a project-to-project basis.

In order to save time, money, and frustration, we recommend that you buy quality tools and equipment at the outset. Taken care of properly, they should provide many years of service.

The tool and equipment needs have been organized into two categories: basic tools needed for most repairs and simple projects, and additional tools for more ambitious projects, especially those involving carpentry skills.

You will find a selection of electrical tools and equipment at many home center stores and hardware outlets.

The Basic Tools

- **Continuity tester** or **voltage tester.**
- **Multipurpose wire stripper.** Removes insulation without damaging wire. Some strippers also cut and bend wire.
- **Needle-nose pliers.** Excellent for bending tight loops in wire to go around terminals.
- **Lineman's pliers.** These pliers have flat jaws used to bend, pull, twist, and grip wires. Some have wire and cable cutters.
- **Set of standard screwdrivers.**
- **Set of Phillips screwdrivers.**
- **Pocket knife** or **utility knife.**
- **Adjustable wrench.** Buy either an 8- or 9-inch wrench for tightening nuts and connectors.
- **Cable insulation ripper.** Removes cable insulation.
- **Electric solder gun.**
- **Multitester** for circuit tests.
- **Wooden rule** or **tape measure.**
- **Hacksaw.**

Additional Tools

Many electrical projects require carpentry tools. The tools frequently needed are listed below.

- **Locking pliers.** Used to grip and hold wires, tighten bolts, and pull cable through conduit and holes.
- **Diagonal, cable, or side cutters.** Used to cut wires in cramped quarters, such as outlet boxes.
- **Adjustable pliers.** Used to handle locknuts and cable connectors.
- **Variable-speed portable electric drill** with several hole-saw, masonry, and wood bits.
- **Wood chisel set; cold chisel.**
- **Portable electric saber saw.**
- **Carpenter's level.**
- **Hammer.**
- **Compass (keyhole) saw.**
- **Fish tape.** Used to pull wires through finished walls and ceilings.
- **Electrical Tape.**
- **Gloves.**

Stripping, Cutting, and Twisting Wires

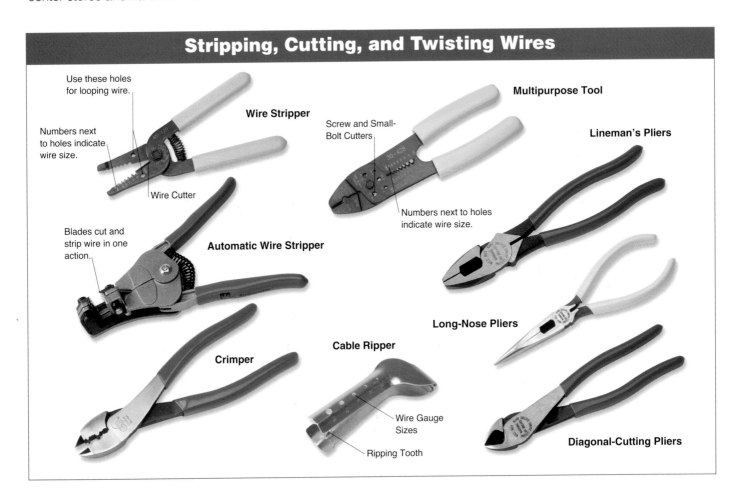

Use these holes for looping wire.

Numbers next to holes indicate wire size.

Wire Stripper

Wire Cutter

Blades cut and strip wire in one action.

Automatic Wire Stripper

Crimper

Screw and Small-Bolt Cutters

Multipurpose Tool

Numbers next to holes indicate wire size.

Cable Ripper

Wire Gauge Sizes

Ripping Tooth

Lineman's Pliers

Long-Nose Pliers

Diagonal-Cutting Pliers

Testing Circuits

Neon Circuit Tester. Use the two probes on a circuit tester to check for live voltage in a circuit. The neon bulb will light if the circuit is live. You can also use the tester to verify that the power to a circuit has been turned off before you work on it.

Receptacle Analyzer. Use a receptacle analyzer to identify faults in receptacle wiring: simply plug the device into the outlet being tested; then read the lighting pattern made by the three bulbs on the analyzer. Different combinations of lighted and unlighted bulbs indicate specific problems with the wiring, such as hot and neutral wires connected in reverse.

Multi-tester. An analog or digital multi-tester, or multimeter, is required to measure voltage and current, as well as to make continuity and resistance checks in switches, fixtures, low-voltage transformers, and other electrical devices.

Continuity Tester. A continuity tester is powered by its own battery, which is used to generate an electrical current through an attached wire and clamp. It must only be used when the power to a circuit is turned off. The tester is especially useful for determining whether or not a cartridge fuse has blown. You can test this type of fuse by touching the tester clamp and probe to the opposite end caps of the fuse. A lighted bulb indicates a working fuse, an unlighted bulb means that the fuse has blown and is in need of replacement. The tester can also be used to detect faults and current interruptions in switches and other types of electrical equipment.

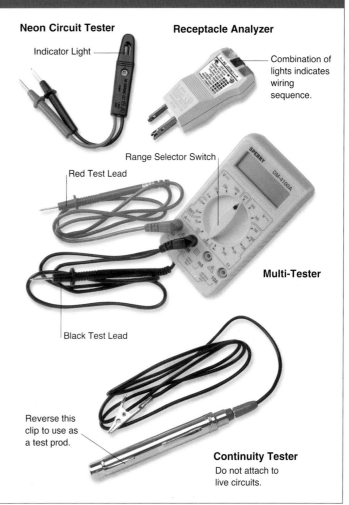

Neon Circuit Tester — Indicator Light

Receptacle Analyzer — Combination of lights indicates wiring sequence.

Range Selector Switch
Red Test Lead
Black Test Lead
Multi-Tester

Reverse this clip to use as a test prod.

Continuity Tester
Do not attach to live circuits.

Safety

Electrician's Gloves. For electrical work you should use a pair of insulated electrician's gloves, rather than using ordinary work gloves. Some high-voltage gloves can protect you up to 20,000 volts, while low-voltage gloves are sufficient for up to 1,000 volts.

Safety Glasses. When doing electrical work of any kind, you should always wear safety glasses or goggles. A sudden spark or a bit of clipped wire could shoot out and burn or scratch your eye. When drilling overhead, it is important to wear safety

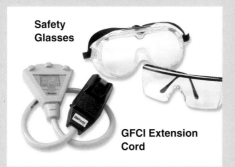

Safety Glasses

GFCI Extension Cord

goggles to protect your eyes from falling debris.

Extension Cords. Because you should never plug a power tool into an electrical circuit unless it is ground-fault protected, a GFCI extension cord can literally be a lifesaver if a tool malfunctions and short-circuits to the housing while you are using it. A 3-foot extension cord with GFCI protection built in is ideal because of its portability. It is sold at most electrical wholesalers and retailers. Use, at minimum, a 12-gauge heavy-duty extension cord to allow your high-voltage tools to obtain maximum voltage, which prolongs their life. Under-gauged extension cords can be a fire hazard.

Ladders. Always use nonconductive wood or fiberglass ladders. Aluminum ladders can be an electrician's nightmare. Should you accidentally cut into a hot wire, you must be insulated from ground—not connected to it. Always wear rubber-soled shoes and electrician's gloves to serve as additional insulators. Brace the ladder by hammering stakes into the ground.

1 Wiring Basics

chapter 2

materials & equipment

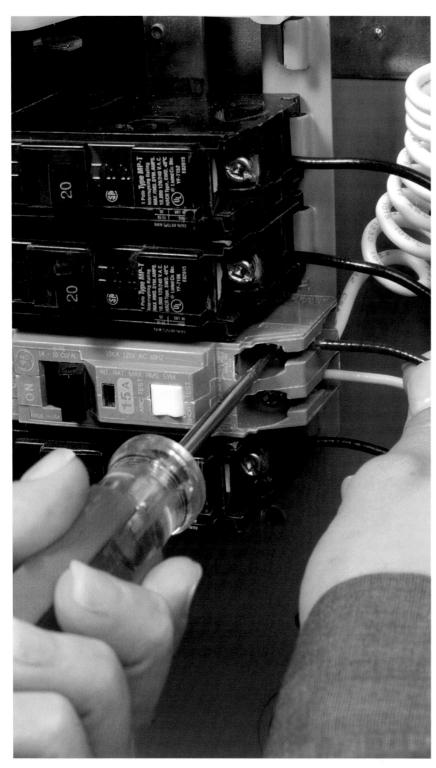

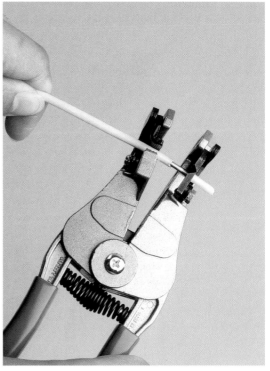

EVEN IF YOU HAVE THE PROPER TOOLS to do your own electrical work, you are only half-prepared for the task. You must also have the right materials and equipment. Plan your electrical work on paper so that you will know exactly what to purchase—from the service panel and electrical boxes to the receptacles, switches, and fixtures. First, you must determine what you're installing and how much power it requires. Then you can decide what categories and quantities of wire to buy; how many circuit breakers and at what amperage; whether or not conduit or cable will be used, and what type; and the accessories needed to connect and fasten wires, conduit, cable, and other materials. Carefully identifying everything you need in advance saves time, money, and effort.

Wires and Cables

Types and Designations

Technically, the metallic material through which electric current flows is called a conductor. In practical terms, most people call it wire. Wire is designated as bare or insulated, stranded or solid, single or multiple, sheathed in cable or encased in insulated cord. In residential work, most wires made of a solid conductive material, such as copper, are encased and protected in plastic insulation. Cables usually consist of two or more insulated wires wrapped together in a second protective layer of plastic sheathing. If the cable includes a grounding wire, it can be insulated, bare, or covered copper wire. Cable is commonly sold boxed in precut lengths. Stranded wires are typically enclosed in an insulating jacket, called a cord. Flexible cord is sometimes precut and packaged but is usually sold off the roll. Whether on a roll or precut, conductors are always sold by the linear foot.

Aluminum and copper-clad aluminum wires have also been used in the past, in addition to copper, as conductive materials. For any electrical work you do, you should use only the kind of wire that is already installed in your home. To find out which kind of wire you have, check the cable type at the main service panel by reading the designation printed on the plastic sheathing. (See table "American Wire Gauges," page 8.)

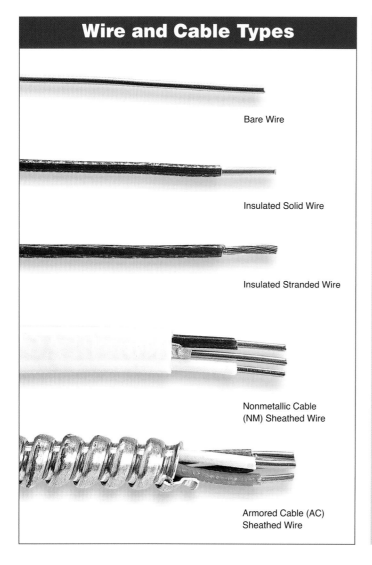

Wire and Cable Types

Bare Wire

Insulated Solid Wire

Insulated Stranded Wire

Nonmetallic Cable (NM) Sheathed Wire

Armored Cable (AC) Sheathed Wire

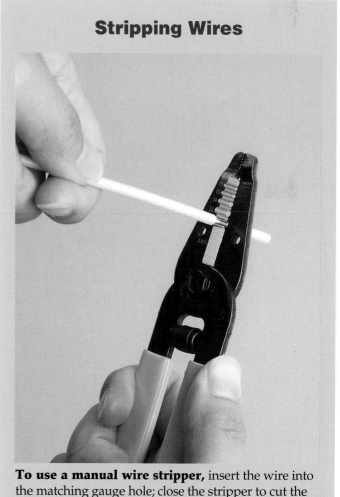

Stripping Wires

To use a manual wire stripper, insert the wire into the matching gauge hole; close the stripper to cut the insulation; and pull it toward the end of the wire.

Cable Coding

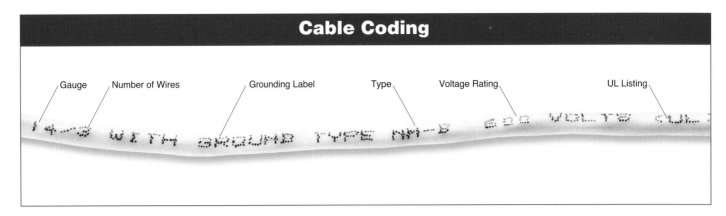

Gauge · Number of Wires · Grounding Label · Type · Voltage Rating · UL Listing

14/3 WITH GROUND TYPE NM-B 600 VOLTS (UL)

For example, consider the following designation: 14/3 WITH GROUND, TYPE NM-B, 600 Volts (UL). The first number shows that the insulated wires inside the cable are 14 gauge (AWG). The second number indicates that the cable contains three wires. "With ground" signifies that a fourth bare copper or green insulated grounding wire is incorporated within the cable. This may simply be designated with the letter G following the number of wires in the cable. "Type NM-B" denotes that the wire is rated at 90 degrees Centigrade (194 degrees Fahrenheit) and is encased in a nonmetallic (plastic) sheathing. Next, the maximum voltage safely carried by the cable is specified as 600 volts. And, finally, the UL notation ensures that the cable is rated as safe for its designated use.

Wire Sizes. You will be concerned mostly with solid-copper wires of 14, 12, and 10 gauge because these are most commonly used for house wiring. Again, the term wire refers to a single conductor. In a cable containing two or more wires, they will all be the same gauge. The AWG system codes the wire diameter as a whole number. The smaller the number, the greater the diameter and current-carrying capacity of the wire. Because wire size recommendations are for copper wires, you must readjust the designation to the next larger size whenever you use aluminum or copper-clad aluminum wire. (12- and 10-gauge aluminum and copper-clad aluminum are no longer manufactured and are not available.)

Color Coding

In addition to the markings on plastic wire insulation, wires are coded by color. Black wires are always hot, as are the red, blue, and yellow wires. White or gray wires are generally (grounded) neutral, with the exception noted below. Green wires are used for grounding only. In addition to having green insulation, grounding wires may also be bare copper. An exception: when a white wire is combined with a black wire in a two-wire cable, the white wire may be used as a hot wire in a switch loop or in a single 240-volt appliance receptacle. In these cases, the white wire must be wrapped with black electrical tape at visible points to identify it as a hot wire. Two-wire cable has a black and white wire; three-wire cable, white, black, and red; four-wire cable, black, white, red, and blue; and five-wire cable, white, black, red, blue, and yellow.

Wire terminal screws are also coded by color. Neutral wires are typically connected to silver or white; grounding or bonding (ensuring a continuously conductive path) wires to green; and hot wires to brass or copper. In a three-way switch, the common (com) wire is usually connected to a screw with a dark finish.

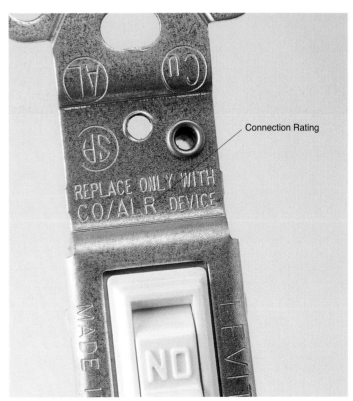

Connection Rating

Connect aluminum wire only to receptacles or switches approved for it and clearly marked with the letters CO/ALR.

Insulation Categories

Wire comes in a variety of insulation types. Be sure that you select the appropriate type for the use and location you have in mind by checking local codes. The most common insulation categories used in residential wiring are THHN, THW, and THWN. The T stands for ordinary thermoplastic insulated cable. You will probably use more of this than any other type of cable. The letter H specifies wire that is heat resistant. A double H indicates wire that can operate at a higher temperature (up to 194 degrees Fahrenheit) than wire designated with a single letter H. The W denotes wire that can be used in dry, damp, or wet locations. The letter N (nylon) specifies that the wire also resists gasoline and/or oil.

Wire Types. THHN wire has flame-retardant, heat-resistant insulation specified for both dry and damp locations. The absence of a W, however, means that the wire is not approved for wet locations. Because nylon insulation is thinner than other kinds of plastic insulation, THHN wire is often used to fit more wires into a conduit. THW wire is flame retardant, and heat and moisture resistant. THWN wire also resists gasoline and oil. Both THW and THWN can be used in dry, damp, or wet locations. They are commonly used in place of THHN in conduit. Another type of wire, XHHW, is often used for service entrance (SE) cable in wet areas instead of THWN. The X indicates that the wire insulation is a flame-retardant, synthetic polymer.

Cable Sheathing Insulation. Indoor house circuits are usually wired using nonmetallic (NM) cable, which is wire contained in a plastic sheathing that's labeled with its specific use. This flexible cable is sometimes known by its trade name, Romex. NM cable contains insulated neutral and power wires and a bare grounding wire. It is used in dry locations only. Each wire is individually wrapped in plastic insulation that is color-coded according to the type of wire inside. Hot wires are typically wrapped in black and neutral wires in white. Grounding wires are either wrapped in green or bare.

The wires in NM cable for common receptacle, light, and small appliance circuits are usually 12/2g or 14/2g. Wire a 20-amp circuit with 12/2g cable. Larger appliance circuits require larger wire sizes. For example, a 30-amp clothes dryer requires 10/3g cable. (See the table, "Representative Loads and Circuits for Residential Equipment," page 20, for more information.)

If a cable is designated type UF (underground feeder and branch-circuit cable), this means that it is suitable for use in wet locations, including direct burial underground. UF cable can be used in place of wire in conduit in some areas and is permitted for interior wiring in place of Type NM cable (NEC Section 340.10). Check local code requirements. The distinguishing characteristic of this type of cable is that the individually insulated wires are embedded in solid, water-resistant plastic.

Cord Insulation. Wire designated as cord differs from cable. The type of wires sheathed in cord are stranded wires. The sheathing usually consists of some type of plastic, rubber, or cloth insulation. Zip cord, for example, contains two wires, usually 18 gauge, encased in a neoprene, synthetic, or other rubberlike insulation. A thin strip of this insulation between the wires is all that holds them together. You can easily separate the wires by pulling, or zipping, them apart. Cord is used primarily for lamps, small appliances, and other wires that have plugs or receptacles attached to one or both ends of the cord. Never use them for fixed-location appliances.

Aluminum Concerns. Be extremely cautious if you use aluminum wire. Though commonly used for heavy appliance circuits, aluminum wire requires special attention in switches and receptacles. Don't use aluminum wire where copper wire is designated. If aluminum wire is used in a device designed for copper wire, the wire will expand and contract as it heats and cools, eventually working loose from the terminal screws. This will create a dangerous situation and may result in an electrical fire. If your home contains copper-clad aluminum wiring, do not add aluminum wiring to it. Instead, use copper wires. If your home has aluminum wire, check whether the switches and receptacles are marked CO/ALR (rated to be connected to aluminum). If the switches and receptacles do not bear this marking, replace them with those that do. Be careful, too, when working with single-strand aluminum wire because it breaks easily. Also, never connect aluminum wire to a back-wired switch or receptacle that uses push-in terminals. Aluminum wire must always be connected to terminal screws (NEC Section 110.14). Note, too, that you can buy UL-listed crimp and twist-on connectors that are specifically made to connect aluminum to copper wire pigtails. These devices are recommended by the Consumer Product Safety Commission.

Aluminum cable is sometimes used for service-entrance cable and large appliances such as electric ranges and electric furnaces. If large diameter, multi-stranded aluminum cable is used, the ends must be coated with a noncorrosive compound (NEC Section 110.14).

Representative Loads and Circuits for Residential Electrical Equipment

Appliance	Volt/ Amperes	Volts	Gauge/ No. of Wires	Circuit Breaker or Fuse in Amps
Range	12,000	115/230	6/3	60
Built-in oven	4,500	115/230	10/3	30
Range top	6,000	115/230	10/3	30
Dishwasher	1,200	115	12/2	20
Waste-disposal unit	300	115	14 or 12/2	15 or 20
Broiler	1,500	115	12/2	20
Refrigerator	300	115	14 or 12/2	15 or 20
Freezer	350	115	14 or 12/2	15 or 20
Washing machine	1,200	115	12/2	20
Clothes dryer	5,000	115/230	10/3	30
Iron	1,650	115	14 or 12/2	15 or 20
Workbench	1,500	115	12/2	20
Portable heater	1,300	115	12/2	20
Television	300	115	14 or 12/2	15 or 20
Fixed lighting	1,200	115	14 or 12/2	15 or 20
Room air conditioner	1,200	115	14 or 12/2	15 or20
Central air conditioner	5,000	115/230	10/3	30
Sump pump	300	115	14 or 12/2	15 or 20
Forced-air furnace	600	115	14 or 12/2	15 or 20
Attic fan	300	115	12/2	20

Wherever the information is available, use actual equipment ratings. A heavy-duty, fixed-location appliance should generally be on its own circuit. Check the manufacturer's literature to determine circuit and direct connections for any appliance before installing and connecting it to your electrical system.

PRO TIP

Estimating Wire

To estimate the amount of wire or cable you will need for a project, measure the distance between the new switch, receptacle, or fixture box and the main panel where the cable originates. Because you will probably not be going in a straight line, remember to allow for curves and offsets. To be safe, add 1 foot for every junction you will make; then provide a margin of error by adding 20 percent to the total calculated distance.

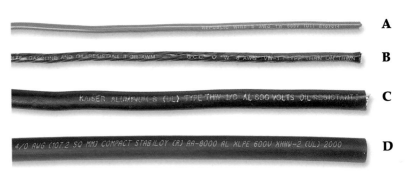

Wire insulation comes in categories, each having a maximum operating temperature and ampacity rating. **A**–TW (Wet Locations); **B**–THHN (Flame and Heat Resistant, Gas/Oil Resistant); THWN (Flame Retardant, Wet Locations, Gas/Oil Resistant); **C**–THW (Flame Retardant, Wet Locations); **D**–XHHW (Service Entrance, Flame and Heat Resistant, Wet Locations)

Splicing Wires

According to the NEC, all wire splices must be enclosed in a switch, receptacle, fixture, or junction box. To make a wire splice, you must first strip insulation from the end of the wires. Although it may be used for this, a utility knife will most likely nick the wire. Instead, use an electrician's wire stripper or multipurpose tool. A wire stripper is operated either manually or automatically. (See "Stripping, Cutting, and Twisting Wires," page 14.) A manual wire stripper requires that you cut the insulation, without cutting the wire, and then pull the cut insulation from the end of the wire. Automatic wire strippers cut and strip the insulation in one motion.

To splice solid wire to solid wire, strip approximately ½ inch of insulation from the end of each wire. Then, using pliers, spirally twist one piece of wire around the other in a clockwise direction. Make the twist tight but not so tight it will cause the wire to break. Cap the splice with a wire connector. (You can also cap the wires without twisting first.) Some people tape around the connector as an added precaution to ensure that the wires will not come out. Splice stranded wires in the same way, but do not strip either type of wire by circling the insulation with cutting pliers and then pulling off the insulation. This will cut into the conductors and cause them to break if they are bent.

To splice a stranded wire to a solid wire, strip the same ½ inch of insulation off the solid wire, but an inch from the stranded wire. Spirally twist the stranded wire clockwise around the solid wire. Cap the splice with a wire connector.

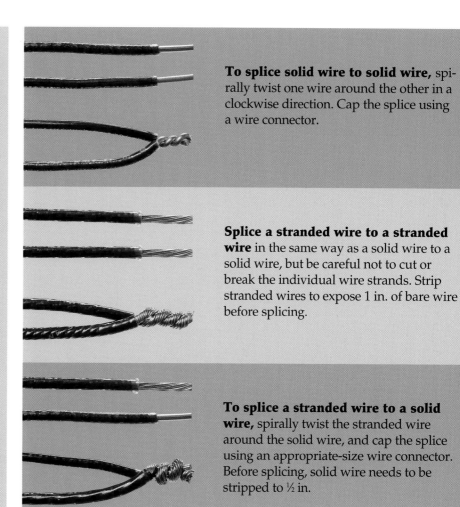

To splice solid wire to solid wire, spirally twist one wire around the other in a clockwise direction. Cap the splice using a wire connector.

Splice a stranded wire to a stranded wire in the same way as a solid wire to a solid wire, but be careful not to cut or break the individual wire strands. Strip stranded wires to expose 1 in. of bare wire before splicing.

To splice a stranded wire to a solid wire, spirally twist the stranded wire around the solid wire, and cap the splice using an appropriate-size wire connector. Before splicing, solid wire needs to be stripped to ½ in.

Wire Connector Ratings

Wire Connector	Color	Minimum		Maximum	
		Gauge	No. Wires	Gauge	No. Wires
	Orange	18	2	14	2
	Yellow	16	2	14	4
	Red	14	2	12	4
				10	3
	Green	Green wire connectors are used for grounding wires only.			

Amperage Ratings for Residential Cable

AWG Size	Insulation Type	Copper		Aluminum/Copper-Clad Aluminum	
		Ordinary Use	Service Entrance	Ordinary Use	Service Entrance
4/0	THW, THWN	230	250	180	200
2/0	THW, THWN	175	200	135	150
1/0	THW, THWN	150	175	120	125
1/0	TW	125	NA	100	NA
1	THW, THWN	130	150	100	110
2	THW, THWN	115	125	90	100
2	TW	95	NA	75	NA
4	THW, THWN	85	100	65	NA
4	TW	70	NA	55	NA
6	THW, THWN	65	NA	50	NA
6	TW	55	NA	40	NA
8	THW, THWN	50	NA	40	NA
8	TW	40	NA	30	NA
10	THW, THWN	35	NA	30	NA
10	TW	30	NA	25	NA
12	THW, THWN	25	NA	20	NA
14	THW, THWN	20	NA	NA	NA

Wires sheathed in thermoplastic insulation (cable) have maximum amperage capacities (ampacities) for which they are rated. The ratings above are for typical residential wires. (NEC Table 310.16)

Wire Ampacity

When selecting wire, consider its ampacity—the amount of current in amperes that a wire can carry safely and continuously under normal conditions, without exceeding its temperature rating. For example, 10-gauge copper wire is rated to carry up to 30 amps; 14-gauge wire, 15 amps. If a wire is too small, it will present a greater-than-normal resistance to the current flowing around it, generating excess heat that could destroy the wire insulation.

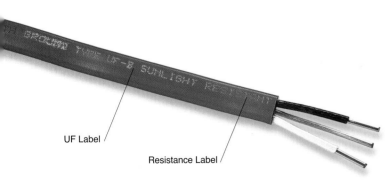

UF Label

Resistance Label

Underground Cable

Underground feeder and branch-circuit cable, or UF cable, can be used for interior wiring wherever NM cable is permitted. However, it is primarily approved for wet locations, such as direct burial underground. To minimize damage to the UF cable, it must be buried a minimum of 1 foot underground if it is a 120-volt circuit and is GFCI-protected. If it is not protected by a GFCI or the circuit exceeds 20 amps, bury it at least 2 feet underground. Check local code regarding direct-burial cable.

The outer sheathing on UF cable is solid thermoplastic, encasing the inner wires completely. This makes it more difficult to separate the wires from the sheathing, as compared with the wires in standard NM cable. The wires inside UF cable are solid and can be spliced in the same way as standard NM wire, but all splices must be made within a watertight box or with approved splicing devices.

Underground feeder and branch-circuit cable is marked with the letters UF. The label also indicates whether the cable is corrosion- and/or sunlight-resistant.

Armored Cable

Wire enclosed in metal sheathing is called armored cable (AC). It is sometimes called by its trade name, BX. Inside the flexible metal sheathing are insulated hot and neutral (grounded) wires and a bare bonding wire. BX is restricted to use indoors in dry locations. It is rarely used in new construction (except in high-rise buildings) because it is expensive and difficult to install. Nevertheless, it is often found in older homes. Metal-clad cable (MC) is a more common type of armored cable. The two cables look alike but are easy to tell apart if you know what to look for. MC cable includes a green grounding wire while AC cable does not. The metal covering on MC cable is not permitted to be the grounding conductor. The wires in MC cable are wrapped in a plastic tape to protect them from chafing against the armored sheathing. Be sure to insert a plastic sleeve between the wires and the armor wherever wires emerge from the armored cable.

For BX, different fittings are used to attach the cable to electrical boxes. All BX fittings work the same way—the cable goes through center of the fitting. The armor itself is connected within the fitting and is held in place by one or two clamps or a twist-on mechanism. As stated, BX is not easy to work with. To splice one BX cable into another requires cutting the armor sheathing without harming the wires inside. This can only be done using a hacksaw or a specialized tool that cuts any type of armored cable. The tool just barely cuts through the armor, which is then twisted to break cleanly, exposing the wires inside. Another drawback to BX is that it cannot turn a tight radius because of the metal sheathing. Too tight a turn will kink the armor, creating a sharp edge. Sharp edges are also created wherever armored cable is cut. This is why it is so important to always install a protective sleeve on the cut ends of the cable to protect the wires inside.

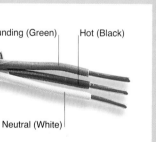

Armored cable (AC) is sometimes called by its trade name, BX. It consists of hot, neutral, and grounding wires in a protective metal (armor) sheathing.

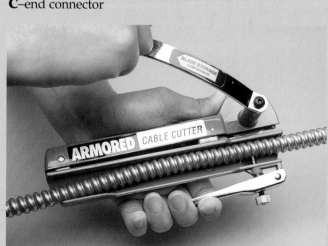

A–squeeze connectors; **B**–90-deg. squeeze connector; **C**–end connector

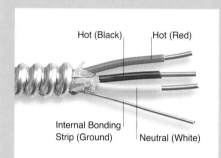

Metal-clad (MC) cable is similar to AC cable, but the wires are wrapped in plastic tape instead of paper.

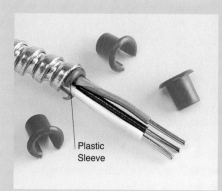

All types of armored cable require a plastic sleeve placed between the sharp metal edges of the cut cable and the emerging wires.

To cut armored cable easily, use a specialized cutting tool. Insert the cable in the tool, and turn the knob clockwise to tighten down on and cut the armor.

Nonmetallic Cable

Nonmetallic (NM) cable is the most common type of cable used in residential work (also known by the trade name Romex). NM cable consists of wires encased in a thermoplastic sheathing. The wires include one or more hot wires, a neutral wire, and a grounding wire. The most common type is two wires with a ground—one hot wire in black insulation, one neutral in white, and a bare copper grounding wire. Three-wire cable is commonly used for house circuits to wire three-way switching or where an extra hot wire is needed, such as for wiring a switch-operated outlet. The third wire is typically encased in red insulation. In some cases, the grounding wire in NM cable may not be included, particularly true of older-style NM cable (prior to 1960).

When you work with NM cable, be sure to avoid two common errors: first, putting a kink in the wires by bending the cable too sharply and, second, damaging the cable sheathing by pulling it through too small an opening. A kink may damage the copper wire inside the cable and can cause it to overheat and create a fire hazard. This also applies to working with the individual wires—never bend them at a right angle but rather bend them gradually. As for sheathing, if it is torn by pulling it through a tight opening, around a sharp turn, or getting it caught on something, the cable may be taped as long as the insulation on the individual wire within the cable is not damaged. Otherwise it must be replaced.

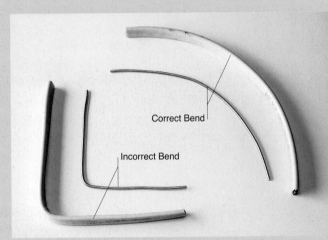

Correct Bend

Incorrect Bend

To prevent damage to wires, never bend individual wires or NM cable at a sharp angle.

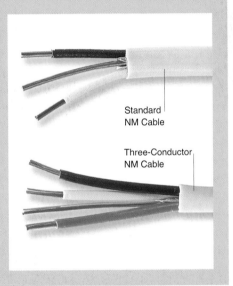

Standard NM Cable

Three-Conductor NM Cable

A standard NM cable contains two insulated wires and one bare copper grounding wire. The hot wire is encased in black insulation and the neutral in white. In a three-conductor NM cable, the additional hot wire is encased in red insulation.

PRO TIP

Removing NM Cable Sheathing

To remove the sheathing on NM cable, insert the cable into a cable ripper, and squeeze the cutting point into the flat side of the cable 8 to 10 inches from the end. Pull lengthwise down the center of the cable. Because the center wire is the bare grounding wire, if you accidentally cut too far into the cable you will not be likely to cut into the insulation on the conductor wires. Peel back the thermoplastic sheathing and the paper wrapping.

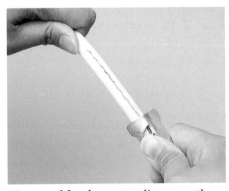

Use a cable ripper to slice open the center of the sheathing on NM cable. This will protect the insulated wires from being cut.

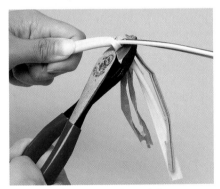

Pull back 8 to 10 in. of the sheathing; then cut away the paper wrapping and excess sheathing, using diagonal cutting pliers.

Service Panels

Types and How They Work

The service-entrance panel (SEP) is the main house panel. It serves two primary purposes. First, the main panel is the only location in or outside the house where all electrical power can be cut off at once. Every adult member of your household should know the location of this panel and how to cut the power in case of an emergency. Second, the main panel is the distribution point and protection center for all of the circuits. All the branch circuits, ones that go to the receptacles, switches, and appliances throughout your house, originate here.

Under the panel cover, circuit breakers, and wires are two copper or aluminum strips. These are the power buses, called hot buses. Each bus is connected to a hot incoming main cable. The circuit breakers are all plugged into these two buses, which provide the breakers with power. Neutral and grounding wires from each circuit are connected to the aluminum neutral/grounding buses on each side of the hot buses. Dead center in the upper part of the panel is a very large breaker, called the main breaker. This breaker controls all of the house power. Its purpose is to monitor the current being drawn, opening the circuit when there is a short or an overload. It also provides manual control over the house power.

Panel Sizes. A typical house panel may provide 100, 150, or 200 amps. Today, 200 amps is most common, although larger all-electric-power homes may use up to 400 amps. Your house's power capacity is noted either on the panel or on the main breaker.

Panels rated for the same maximum current capacity, such as 200 amps, are subdivided by the number of breakers they can hold. The maximum number of breakers a residential panel can hold is 42 breakers plus the main breaker. This type of panel is called a 42/42 panel. The first number refers to the number of full-size breakers the panel can hold, and the second number refers to the maximum number of breakers the panel can hold regardless of breaker type. The next listing is a 40/40 panel. In a listing such as 30/40 panel, the panel can hold only 30 full-size breakers. To increase the panel to 40 breakers, half-size breakers must be used. It is preferable to use full-size breakers for safety reasons. Smaller panels may hold a maximum of 20 or 30 breakers. Avoid these panels because they will not provide breaker space for future expansion.

Circuit-Breaker Sizes. Individual breakers distribute power from the hot buses to the circuits. A standard-tab hot bus will accept only standard full-size breakers; a split-tab hot bus can accept either twin (dual) or half-size breakers. A twin breaker consists of two breakers installed within the space usually occupied by a single breaker. Use breakers and panel boxes from the same manufacturer.

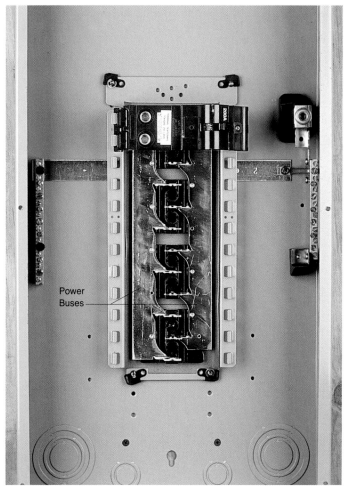

Power Buses

The service-entrance, or main, panel is both the entry and distribution point for all the circuits in your home. If the panel cover, breakers, and wires were removed, you would see the two power buses into which all of the circuit breakers are plugged. The main breaker, at the top, controls power entering the hot buses. Turn off the power by moving the handle to the off position on the main disconnect. Breakers trip automatically if the circuit shorts or is overloaded.

Circuit Breaker Screw

To install an individual breaker, left, first turn off the main power; then hook the notched end onto the hot bus tab, and snap it firmly in place. A circuit's hot wire, right, is secured beneath a circuit breaker screw. Insert the bare wire end in the terminal hole, and tighten the screw over the wire.

Circuit Breakers

Circuit breakers have replaced fuses as the preferred type of circuit protection. Technically, they are called molded-case circuit breakers, or MCCBs. Circuit breakers use a two-part system for protecting circuit wiring. When a small overload is on the circuit, a thermal strip will heat up and open, or trip, the circuit. When a massive amount of current comes through very quickly, as in a ground fault or short circuit, an electromagnet gives the thermal strip a boost. The greater the amount of trip current, the faster the breaker will trip.

The most important advantage circuit breakers have over fuses is that they can be easily reset; you don't have to buy a new one every time an appliance draws excessive current. When a breaker is tripped, it won't work unless you throw it all the way to the off position before you turn it back on again. Another characteristic of circuit breakers is that they are air-ambient-compensated—the hotter the air around them gets, the sooner they will trip. For example, if all the circuit breakers around a specific 20-amp breaker are running hot, because of an excessive flow of current, the 20-amp breaker may trip at only 18 amps.

Residential circuit breakers typically range in size from 15 to 60 amps, increasing at intervals of 5 amps. Single-pole breakers rated for 15 to 20 amps control most 120-volt general-purpose circuits. Double-pole breakers rated for 20 to 60 amps control 240-volt circuits.

Standard circuit breakers are universal and have clips on the bottom that snap onto the hot-bus tabs in the panel box. Contact with the hot bus brings power into the breaker. Be aware, however, that some manufacturers make breakers with wire clips that mount on the side. These clips slide over the tab on the hot bus, requiring you to remove one or more of the other breakers to get at the one you want.

Common Breaker Types. In addition to single- and double-pole breakers, quad breakers, GFCI breakers, and surge-protection devices are also available. Single-pole breakers supply power to 120-volt loads such as receptacle and light circuits. A hot black or red wire is usually connected to the breaker. Single-pole breakers come full size or in a two-in-one configuration (twin). The latter type will only fit into a panel having a split-tab hot bus.

Double-pole breakers provide power to 240-volt appliances such as electric water heaters and dryers. If a standard NM cable is used as the conductors, both the black and the white wire are connected to the breaker. The white wire must be marked with black tape at both ends. Larger double-pole circuits have two black conductors in the circuit.

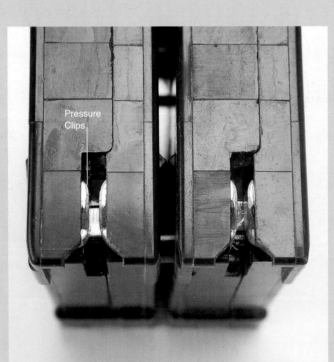

Two contacts, or pressure clips, on the underside of a circuit breaker snap over a hot-bus tab in the main panel. These contacts bring power into the breaker.

An AFCI breaker will shut down a circuit when it detects an intermittent arc of current, such as an arc caused by a loose connection.

Specialty Breakers. A quad breaker falls within the half-size breaker family and can contain several configurations within one unit. It may, for example, contain two double-pole circuits, such as a double-pole 30-amp and a double-pole 20-amp circuit; it may have two single-pole circuits and one double pole; or it may provide power to some other combination of circuits. The advantage of a quad breaker is that it takes up half the space of a standard breaker. The panel, though, must be specially designed to accept quad breakers.

A GFCI circuit breaker fits into the main panel just like a standard circuit breaker. On its face is a test button but no reset. If properly installed, pressing the test button places a deliberate, preset current imbalance (6 milliamperes) on the line to verify that the breaker will trip when there is an unintended imbalance. When tripped, the breaker arm will go to a halfway off position, cutting power to the circuit.

Arc-fault circuit interrupter (AFCI) breakers are required on branch circuits that supply power to all living areas of a home. These devices look like GFCI breakers. Their purpose is to detect an arcing situation, such as loose or corroded connections or damaged insulation on a wire, and then shut down the current on the circuit before the heat generated by the arc causes a fire.

A surge-protection device, which protects an entire panel, can be confusing at first glance. You will see a device that looks like a double-pole body. This type of device also has two lights that glow when power is applied to the panel. But a surge-protection device connects to the buses in the same way as any other circuit breaker.

Limits. Circuit breakers are limited in protecting wires, and therefore life and property. Breakers other than GFCI cannot prevent electric shock, for instance. Although breakers trip at 15 amps and above, it only takes about 0.06 amp to electrocute someone. Circuit breakers cannot prevent overheating of a fixture or appliance or other device, and they can't prevent low-level faults. For a breaker to trip, a fault must occur when enough current is being demanded to exceed the trip current of the breaker. Breakers cannot trip fast enough to completely block lightning surges from entering the house circuits. They cannot prevent fires within appliances. Circuit breakers are meant to save the wiring to the appliance—not the appliance itself.

Breaker Types

A single-pole breaker is the most prevalent type in residential use. It will power anything that requires 120-volt current.

A double-pole breaker is used with a 240-volt appliance, such as a 20-amp baseboard heater or a 30-amp clothes dryer.

Use a quad breaker to serve two double-pole circuits in the same space as one standard double-pole breaker.

A GFCI circuit breaker will cut power to a circuit when it is tripped by an imbalance in current flow hrough the wires.

A surge-protection device provides protection for an entire service panel and simply installs in place of two single-pole breakers.

2 Materials & Equipment

Fuses

The fuse was the most common type of circuit protection in homes prior to World War II. Fuses are still used in many older homes. The two most common types of fuses are the plug, or glass fuse, and the cartridge fuse. Plug fuses control 120-volt circuits and are commonly available in sizes ranging from 15 to 30 amps. Inside a plug fuse is a metal strip that extends from the fuse's center contact to the threaded base. The narrow portion of the strip is called the element. If the circuit is overloaded, the element will burn, disconnecting the circuit and blowing the fuse. Cartridge fuses for residential use control 240-volt circuits and typically range in size from 30 to 100 amps. The element in a cartridge fuse runs down the center of the cartridge and is surrounded by a fireproof material that resembles sand.

Most fuse panels in use today are probably quite old. It is rather common for fuse boxes like these to require troubleshooting. Loose connections in an old fuse holder may produce enough heat to instantaneously vaporize a fuse element. If a fuse or fuse holder is discolored (brown or black) or if burn or melt spots are obvious, it is recommended that you replace the entire fuse panel with a circuit-breaker panel.

Replacing a fuse with another one that has a higher amperage rating can allow excessive current on a circuit wire, damaging the wire insulation and possibly causing a fire. Type S fuses were developed to solve this problem. Because each fuse size has a different base threading design, only one size can be installed in a particular circuit.

Sometimes a fuse may blow because of a momentary surge of power coming into the electrical system. Another type of fuse, called a time-delay fuse, can withstand this kind of power surge without blowing.

Fuse Overload. When a circuit is overloaded and the fuse element melts, disconnecting, or opening, the circuit, the damage to the element can be seen easily by looking through the fuse glass.

An overload occurs whenever the amount of current drawn by one or more fixtures or appliances exceeds the fuse rating. You determine a fuse rating by the gauge of wire that the fuse protects. In the absence of a fuse (or other circuit protection) or when devices use too much current, the wire becomes overheated, damaging the insulation, possibly causing a fire. Some fuses can

An obsolete fuse box is commonly found in older homes. Such boxes are frequently in need of troubleshooting or replacement.

Hot Wire (Black)

Neutral Wire (White)

When a black hot wire comes into contact with a white neutral wire, a short circuit results. This often occurs when wires are poorly connected.

be reset rather than replaced (not recommended). Be careful that this type of fuse fits properly into your panel and does not interfere with door closure.

Short Circuits and Ground Faults. A short circuit occurs when a hot wire touches a neutral wire. This sometimes happens by accident when wires are improperly connected. It may also happen when an appliance malfunctions or a circuit is improperly wired. In any case, a short circuit will result in a massive current flow through the fuse, causing the element to destruct and open the circuit. When this happens, the view through the glass on a plug fuse will be obscured by a black/silver discoloration. If this happens to a cartridge fuse, however, it will reveal no visible sign that it has been blown. You must test the fuse using a multi-tester to be sure the fuse has blown

A ground fault occurs when a hot wire touches a grounding wire or any grounded surface. As in a short circuit, massive current flow will cause the fuse to blow. Unfortunately, you cannot tell a short circuit from a ground fault by looking at the blown fuse.

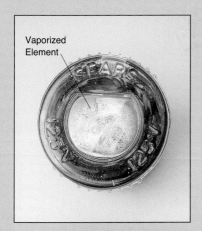

Vaporized Element

When a short circuit or ground fault occurs, a massive amount of current will surge through a glass fuse, causing the element to be vaporized.

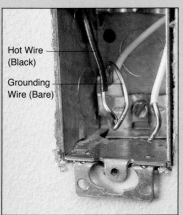

Hot Wire (Black)

Grounding Wire (Bare)

When a hot wire touches a grounding wire or grounded metal appliance frame, a ground fault will occur.

Fuse Types

GLASS FUSES

Element

Blown Fuse

Glass, or plug, fuses are found in older homes. Replacing a fuse with one of larger capacity is a fire hazard. On a correctly sized fuse, a metal element inside the fuse will burn and blow out (right), indicating a circuit overload or short circuit if the current exceeds capacity.

CARTRIDGE FUSES

A 60-amp cartridge fuse may be used as the main fuse in an older home. Cartridge fuses range from 30 to 100 amps. A cartridge fuse contains an element not unlike that in a glass fuse, except that it is embedded in nonflammable material (right).

TYPE S FUSES

Base Threading

The Type S fuse was designed to replace the standard glass fuse. Each Type S fuse size has a different base-threading configuration (right) to prevent a homeowner from installing a high-amp fuse in a low-amp fuse socket.

TIME-DELAY FUSES

Some glass fuses are designed to withstand a temporary surge in power without blowing. This type of fuse should be marked "time-delay" on the edge.

Electrical Boxes

Types and Capacities

Electrical boxes are used for a variety of purposes, such as holding receptacles and switches, housing wire junctions, and supporting ceiling fans and lights. Many types of boxes are made for different purposes, and they can be metal or nonmetallic (plastic or fiberglass). Today, plastic boxes are the type most commonly used. However, metal boxes are still found in many homes. Check code requirements before installing electrical boxes. Plastic boxes have the advantages of low cost and simplicity of installation.

Electrical boxes come in standard shapes for each type of use. For example, they may be shallow for furred walls, wider for ganged arrangements, or waterproof for outdoor applications. Be sure to use the right box. No matter what the purpose, though, every box must be covered and accessible. It is also important not to use a box that is too small for the size and number of wires it will house. An electrical box can hold only a limited number of wires. Determining how many wires a box can safely hold can be complicated. Requirements change as the code changes.

Although plastic boxes are labeled according to the number of wires they can house, and/or their size in cubic inches, metal boxes are not. Cubic-inch capacities for a variety of metal boxes are listed in NEC Table 314.16(A). The safest way to overcome this problem is by purchasing the deepest box that will fit into your stud wall—one that is 3¼ to 3½ inches deep. For a single-gang box, this will provide 20.3 cubic inches of wiring space. Use common sense, and don't overcrowd any box. (See "Maximum Wires in a Box," page 44.)

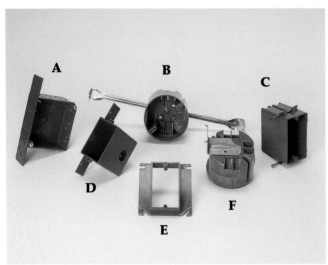

Nonmetallic boxes: **A**–MP bracket square box; **B**–adjustable ceiling box; **C**–receptacle and switch box; **D**–MP bracket switch box; **E**–raised device cover; **F**–JP bracket ceiling box

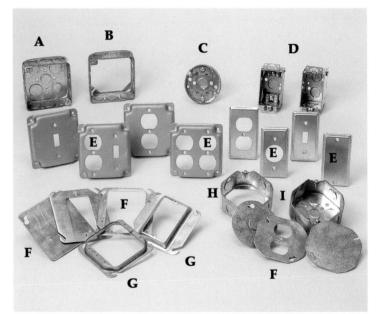

Electrical boxes come in many shapes and sizes for different purposes and are made of metal, plastic, or fiberglass. Though use of plastic boxes is widespread today, they don't meet code requirements for some jobs. Splice boxes are required for all wire junctions.
Metallic boxes: A–square; **B**–box extension; **C**–ceiling pan box; **D**–receptacle and switch boxes; **E**–exposed box cover plates; **F**–concealed box flat plates; **G**–raised device covers; **H**–box extension; **I**–octagonal box

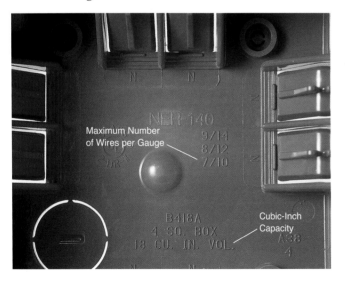

The inside of a nonmetallic electrical box, left, is labeled with the cubic-inch capacity of the box as well as the maximum permitted number of wires per gauge.

Plastic Boxes

The most common type of plastic box is the single-gang, nail-on box. It has two integral nails that fasten it to stud framing. This type of box is commonly used in new construction and is available in several depths—the deepest having the greatest capacity.

Box Placement. When attaching nail-on boxes to studs, leave enough of the box edge protruding to bring the box flush with the finished wall. If you don't know the depth of the finished wall, use an adjustable box. Once installed, this box can be moved in and out on a slider to match the finished wall depth. The slider also allows you to change from a single box to a double without ripping apart the wall. You just unscrew and remove the single box, cut the opening to the new size, and insert the new box on the slider.

All plastic boxes must be installed carefully because they can be easily damaged. If a plastic box is hit with a hammer or if nails are driven in too far, the box will distort or break. Drive nails until they are snug, but no farther.

Ceiling Boxes. Ceiling pan boxes are typically used for ceiling fixtures. Named for its shape, a ceiling pan box may be designed to hold a fixture, such as a ceiling fan/light, weighing up to 35 pounds. If this is the case, it will be labeled. This type of box can be screwed or nailed directly into a ceiling joist. It is preferable, though, to screw the box into a wooden support such as a flat 2x6 spanning between two joists. A box having integral nails can break easily and will not support weight well. A fixture that weighs more than 50 pounds, such as a chandelier (35 for a paddle fan), cannot be suspended from a box. Instead, it must be supported independently from the box. Another way to mount an overhead fixture is by using an approved box with an adjustable bar hanger attached to it. Mounted between two overhead joists, this type of box can be positioned anywhere along the bar between the two joists.

Most plastic boxes, regardless of purpose, have internal clips that clamp onto the NM cable where it is inserted into the box. Open these clips using a flat-blade screwdriver before inserting the cable.

Plastic Box Types

Deep Box   Shallow Box

Plastic nail-on boxes are available in many sizes, shallow or deep. Use the deepest box that can fit your space when installing receptacles, switches, and wires.

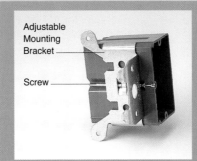

Adjustable Mounting Bracket
Screw

Adjustable boxes provide for variations in finished wall thicknesses, even after they are installed. Turning a screw on the face of the box adjusts it in or out.

Quad   Triple
Double

Multiple-switch boxes—double, triple, and quad. A quad box should be attached to two framing studs, one on each side, to prevent wobbling.

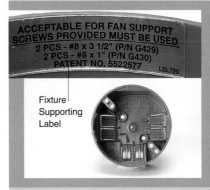

ACCEPTABLE FOR FAN SUPPORT
SCREWS PROVIDED MUST BE USED
2 PCS - #8 x 3 1/2" (P/N G429)
2 PCS - #8 x 1" (P/N G430)
PATENT NO. 5522577   LBL720

Fixture Supporting Label

Ceiling pan boxes for overhead fixtures bolt to framing. If a fixture weighs up to 50 lbs., the box must be marked "For Support"; if it weighs more, it must be supported independently.

Some ceiling-fixture boxes are supported between joists with an adjustable bar hanger. You adjust the fixture location by sliding the box along the bar.

Metal Boxes

Though more expensive and harder to work with than plastic boxes, metal boxes have some advantages. For one, they are available in more configurations than plastic boxes because they have been around longer. Basic boxes include the switch or receptacle box (rectangular) and the fixture or equipment outlet box (square or octagonal). One of the greatest advantages of metal boxes is that they are much stronger than plastic boxes. Because they can stand up to greater abuse, they are suitable for use in exposed locations such as unfinished basements and garages. To accommodate different finished wall thicknesses, some metal boxes have a built-in depth gauge.

Another important advantage is that some metal boxes have removable sides that allow additional boxes to be added, or ganged, to accommodate more than one device. A single-gang box, for instance, can be expanded to become a quad box.

A depth gauge marked on an electrical box tells the installer where to align the box on a framing stud so that its face will be flush with the finished drywall.

Adding Space to a Metal Gangable Box

1. To add space to a gangable box, use a screwdriver to remove the retaining screw on the side of the existing box to be expanded, and take out the side panel.

2. Remove the opposite panel from a second, add-on box.

3. Remove the retaining screw from the open side of the second box, and align the screw slot over the retaining screw on the open side of the first box.

4. Tighten the retaining screw, creating one double-size box.

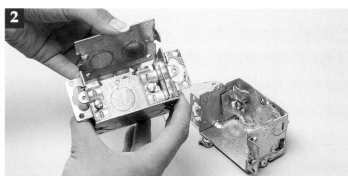

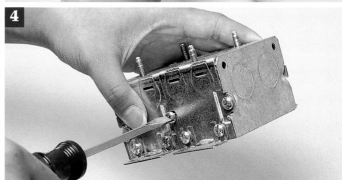

Bringing NM Cable into a Metal Box

To bring NM cable into a metal box, you must first remove one of the knockouts on the box. Some boxes have a pryout built into them that can easily be removed using a flat-blade screwdriver. Others have a circular knockout that must be punched out using a hammer and a screwdriver or knockout punch. Once the knockout hole is open, a cable clamp can be inserted into the opening. The clamp secures the cable in place and protects it from chafing against the sharp metal edges of the box opening.

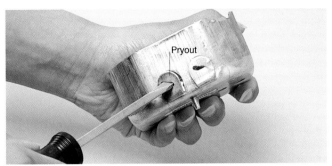

Some metal boxes have pryouts that can be removed using the flat blade of a screwdriver.

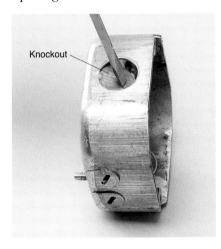

Other boxes have knockouts that must be punched out with a hammer and screwdriver or with a special tool called a knockout punch.

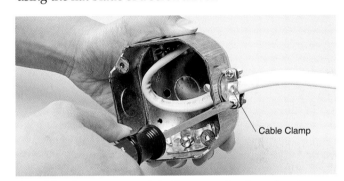

A cable clamp screws into the pryout or knockout opening to secure the cable entering the box and protect it from chafing against the sharp edges of the opening.

Weatherproof Boxes

Boxes mounted outdoors must be watertight. One way to achieve this is by recessing a standard box with a watertight lid in an outside house wall. Another is to mount a watertight box with a watertight lid on the surface of the exterior wall.

The problem with either method is that once the lid is opened, the box is no longer watertight; the interior is exposed. The NEC requires that when unattended equipment is left plugged into an exterior outlet, a special box or lid must be used that will keep the outlet weatherproof even while the plug is in place [Section 406.8(B)].

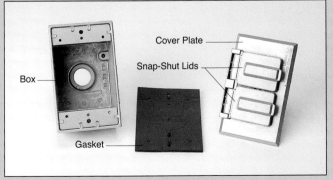

A watertight outdoor-receptacle box has a foam sealing gasket and a cover with snap-shut receptacle lids.

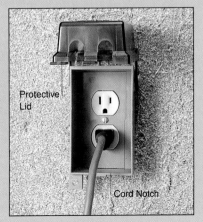

A weatherproof box must remain watertight even while the receptacle is in use. This type of box must have a lid that closes over the plug-in cord.

Special Boxes

Special types of electrical boxes include pancake and cut-in boxes. Pancake boxes are commonly used to mount outside entrance lights. Because of their low silhouette, they can be attached to the surface of an exterior wall yet remain hidden beneath the dome of the exterior light.

Retrofit cut-in boxes are available in metallic and nonmetallic forms. Both types have flat lips, or drywall ears, on the front and some type of adjustable wing on the back. The wings expand outwardly, grabbing the back of the finished wall surface, while the metal ears on the front keep the box from falling into the opening. Metal cut-in boxes are not as popular as fiberglass or plastic because they are more expensive, must be grounded, and often have limited room for wires.

Old-work, or cut-in, boxes are for retrofits and are designed for installation in existing walls. Once inserted into a wall opening, screws are adjusted to expand side wings that grasp the back of finished drywall or plaster. Ceiling cut-in boxes should not be used to support heavy fixtures.

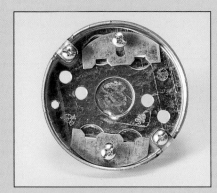

Pancake boxes are aptly named because of their flat, round shape. They contain minimal cubic volume and are designed to fit under the dome of an exterior light.

Screw-Adjustable Wings

Installing a Cut-In Box

To install a receptacle, switch, or ceiling cut-in box, first trace a template of the box on the surface of the wall or ceiling. Using a keyhole or saber saw, cut the opening for the box. Insert the box in the opening; then adjust and tighten the wings against the back of the drywall.

1. Trace a template of the box on the wall or ceiling surface, and cut the opening for the box.

2. Insert the box in the opening, and adjust the side wings.

3. Tighten the adjusting screws to bring the wings firmly against the back of the finished wall (view from inside the wall).

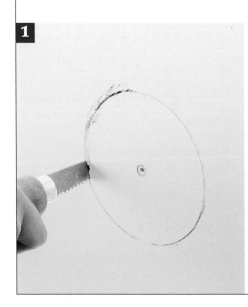

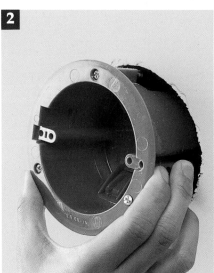

Box Extensions and Mounting Brackets

Box Extensions

Box extensions, or extension rings, are used to add wiring capacity to a box. If a finished ceiling or wall surface lies beyond a box front or more space is needed for wiring within the box, simply add an extension ring. Use a watertight box extension for outdoor work.

Mounting Brackets

Brackets exist for mounting every type of metallic and nonmetallic box under a wide variety of installation conditions. Though some brackets are used for only one purpose, others may be used for several types of boxes. Each bracket type attaches a box differently. An A bracket, for example, attaches to the face and side of a stud, while a B bracket only attaches to the face and a D bracket only to the side of a stud. Metal framing-stud mounting brackets are also available. Other brackets are used for gangable boxes and boxes that must be backset or offset from stud work. Mounting brackets for plastic boxes are available in fewer styles. Because of they are less

durable, nonmetallic boxes are more likely to have nailing spurs than actual brackets. Discuss your wiring plans with your electrical supply retailer to be sure you are getting the right type brackets.

Metal mounting brackets: A–FM bracket; **B**–FA brackets; **C**–A bracket; **D**–S bracket; **E**–J bracket; **F**–long B bracket

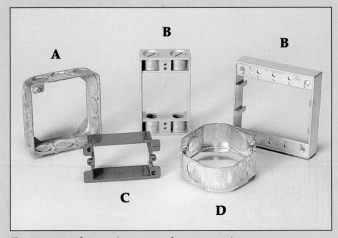

Box extensions: A–square-box extension; **B**–watertight-box extensions; **C**–rectangular-box extension; **D**–octagonal box extension

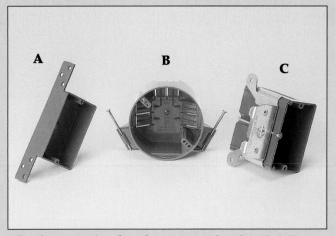

Plastic mounting brackets: A–MP bracket; **B**–WP bracket; **C**–adjustable bracket

Receptacles

Duplex Receptacles

Different types of receptacles are manufactured for a variety of residential purposes. Standard duplex receptacles are the most common type available and are used to power fixtures, appliances, and residential equipment rated for 110 to 125 volts. This type of duplex receptacle has a long neutral slot, a short hot slot, and an arch-shaped grounding hole. This configu-

ration guarantees that a plug can only be inserted into the receptacle one way—so it will be properly polarized and grounded.

Nongrounded Receptacles

Older receptacles have only two slots and no grounding hole. If the two slots are identical, the receptacle is neither grounded nor polarized. If one slot is long and the other short, the receptacle is polarized but not grounded.

Receptacle Types

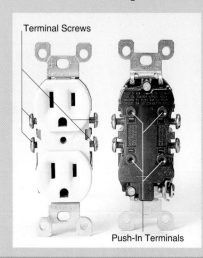

Terminal Screws

Push-In Terminals

Standard duplex receptacles have terminal screws for connecting wires. Some also have push-in terminals where 14-gauge wires can be inserted, but these connect less securely and are not recommended.

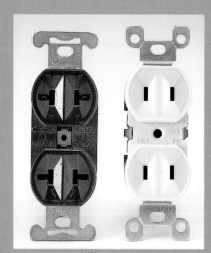

Older receptacles have only two slots. If both are the same size, as in these outlets, the receptacle is neither grounded nor polarized. If one slot is longer than the other, the receptacle is polarized but not grounded.

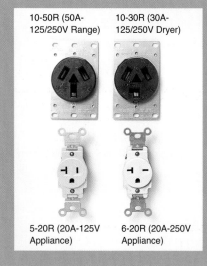

10-50R (50A-125/250V Range)

10-30R (30A-125/250V Dryer)

5-20R (20A-125V Appliance)

6-20R (20A-250V Appliance)

High-voltage appliance receptacles have specific slot configurations that are designed to prevent you from plugging an appliance into the wrong circuit. For new construction, use four-slot range and dryer receptacles.

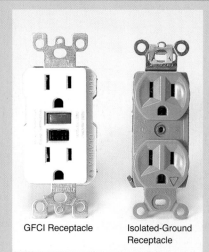

GFCI Receptacle

Isolated-Ground Receptacle

A GFCI receptacle protects the user against electric shock, while an isolated-ground receptacle protects sensitive equipment from power surges.

Appliance Receptacles

Other types of receptacles have slot configurations that limit their use to specific appliances or groups of appliances. For example, the hot slot on a large 20-amp appliance or tool receptacle is T-shaped, while the hot and neutral slots on an air-conditioner receptacle are horizontal instead of vertical. Appliances that draw high currents, such as clothes dryers and ranges, use a single dedicated receptacle. Each type has a slot configuration designated only for the particular appliance being powered. The amperage and voltage are clearly marked on the receptacle, along with the number assigned by the National Electrical Manufacturers Association (NEMA) and the listing mark of the Underwriters Laboratories (UL). The NEMA code ensures that you are buying the correct receptacle for the appliance, and the UL-listing label indicates that the receptacle has passed rigorous testing standards.

Isolated-Ground and GFCI Receptacles

An isolated-ground receptacle is a specialized, orange-colored device. It has an insulated grounding screw and is primarily used to protect sensitive electronic equipment, such as computers, from disruptive or damaging electrical power surges. A GFCI (ground-fault circuit-interrupter) receptacle is a special duplex receptacle that protects you from a fatal electrical shock. When incoming and returning current are unequal, the GFCI cuts off the circuit in a fraction of a second, before you can feel a shock. This type of receptacle is required by code in wet locations, such as bathrooms, kitchens, basements, garages, and outdoors.

Switches

Types and Designations

A switch controls the flow of power in an electrical circuit. When a switch is on, electricity flows through the circuit from its source to the point of use. The standard switch used in residential work is the toggle switch, sometimes called a snap switch. Other types include dimmer, pilot-light, timer, and electronic switches. Switches are further categorized by quality and usage. The standard, or construction grade, switch is rated for 15 amps and is the grade and type most commonly found in homes.

Toggle Switches

Toggle switches have evolved over time. Now you can perform many functions throughout a home with them. A standard, single-pole toggle switch turns a light on from only one location. But switches may also control a circuit from two (three-way switch) or three (four-way switch)

locations. A single-pole switch has two terminal screws. Only this one switch can control the circuit. The hot wire connects to one terminal, and the outgoing wire to the other. A three-way switch has three terminals. One is marked com or "common"; the hot wire connects to this terminal. The other terminals are switch leads. A four-way switch has four terminals. A similar-looking switch, the double-pole switch, is used to control 240-volt appliances and is differentiated from the four-way switch by the on and off markings on the toggle.

Dimmer Switches

A dimmer switch is used to control the brightness, or intensity, of light emitted from a light fixture by increasing or decreasing the flow of electricity to the fixture. Dimmers may have standard toggle switches, rotary dials, sliders, or automatic electronic sensors that respond to the level of ambient light in a room and adjust accordingly. They can be single-pole or three-way switches.

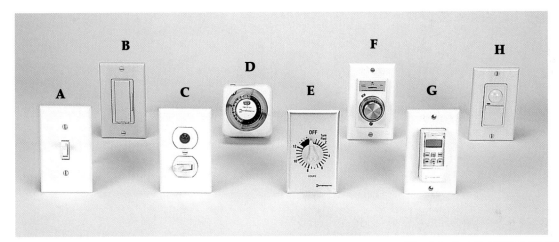

Switches: A–toggle; **B**–large-button toggle; **C**–pilot light; **D**–clock timer; **E**–time delay; **F**–automatic; **G**–programmable; **H**–motion sensor

PRO TIP

Reading a Switch

Switches must be marked with labels that represent different ratings and approvals. These labels convey important information about safety and usage. The designation UND. LAB-INC. LIST, for example, means that the switch has been listed by the Underwriters Laboratories, an independent testing agency. AC ONLY indicates that the switch can only handle alternating current. CO/ALR specifies that the switch can be connected to either copper or aluminum wires. A switch marked CU can be used only with copper and not with aluminum wires. The amp and voltage ratings are given by designations like 15A–120V, which means that the switch is approved for use with circuits that carry 15 amps of current at 120 volts.

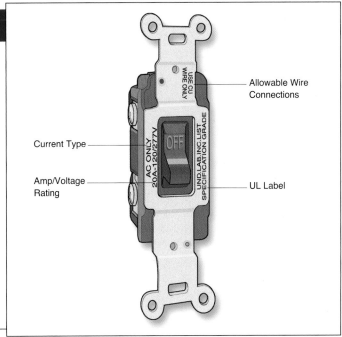

Switch Types

3-Way   4-Way

Single Pole   Double Pole

A single-pole toggle switch operates a light from one location. Other types include double-pole and three- and four-way switches.

Standard toggle switches can be side-wired at screw terminals or back-wired at push-in terminals. Older switches may be front- or end-wired.

Toggle   Dial   Slider

A dimmer switch controls the brightness of light emitted from a bulb. Dimmer switches may have toggle, dial, slide, or automatic controls.

A green or red light will glow on a pilot-light switch to indicate that an appliance or other type of circuit is turned on or active.

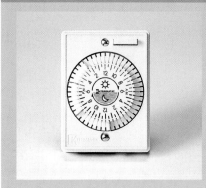

A clock-timer turns a circuit on or off at a set time of day, while a time-delay switch operates a circuit for a set length of time.

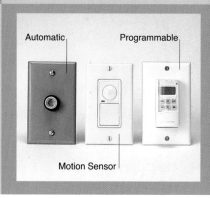

Automatic   Programmable

Motion Sensor

Automatic, motion-sensor, and programmable switches are types of electronic switches. Movement detected by an infrared eye will trigger a motion sensor.

Pilot-Light Switches

Pilot-light switches are usually found on appliances but are especially useful for controlling remote fixtures, like porch, attic, basement, and garage lights, because they can let you know whether or not a light is on or off. When a fixture or appliance is turned on, the pilot light is illuminated.

Timer Switches

Timer switches come in two varieties: clock and time delay. A clock-timer can be set to turn on a fixture or other device at a preset time of day. An example would be a thermostat set to turn down the heat during the day when no one is home. Another example would be a switch that turns on security lights in your home after dark or when you are away on vacation. This type of switch can also be used to operate a lawn-sprinkler system. In contrast, a time-delay switch is designed to allow a fixture or appliance to operate for a set period

of time and then shut off. An example would be a heat lamp or exhaust fan in a bathroom.

Electronic Switches

Electronic switches offer automatic control of lights and other devices. As a matter of safety, they can be overridden by using manual switch levers. An automatic switch allows a user to simply wave a hand in front of the switch to turn it on or off. An infrared beam emitted from the switch detects the movement of the user's hand and activates an electronic signal to operate the switch. A motion-sensor switch operates the same way but is designed for security lighting. When someone or something passes in front of the infrared eye, the light is activated. When the motion ceases, the light will turn itself off after a set period of time has elapsed. Outdoor perimeter or garage lighting is commonly on this type of switch. A programmable switch is a digitally controlled version of the clock-timer.

It can be programmed to turn lights and other devices on and off several times a day at specified or random times. For security, this type of switch is especially advantageous when you are away from home.

Low-Voltage Transformers

Types and Applications

Many types of household fixtures and equipment require much less power to operate than is provided by standard 120-volt house current: door chimes, low-voltage outdoor and pool lights, telephones, antennas, and thermostats are just a few examples. A low-voltage transformer steps down 120-volt house current to 30 volts or less. Some fixtures may come with a built-in transformer that serves only that device. A remote transformer is externally connected and can control several devices. A special weatherproof transformer is used to power low-voltage lighting outdoors. The most common type of transformer used in residential work, however, is a simple box-mounted transformer that attaches to a junction box. Both the supply and device wires are connected to the transformer wires inside the junction box.

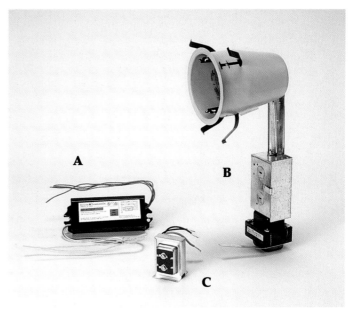

Low-voltage transformers may be installed separately or come as an integral part of a fixture. **A**–remote transformer; **B**–lighting transformer; **C**–device transformer

Raceways

Raceway Application

To an electrician, raceway and conduit are interchangeable terms, but for our purposes a raceway houses surface wiring. This eliminates fishing cable through existing walls, allowing wire to be run along masonry surfaces. Raceways protect cable in enclosed plastic or metal casings. Raceway wiring includes receptacles, switches, and ceiling fixtures. Special connectors turn corners, providing intersections to extend branches. Raceways are grounded by an equipment-grounding conductor, a metal casing, or both. The NEC limits raceway use to dry locations not exposed to physical damage. Raceways are permitted to contain a certain number and size of wires for each intended use.

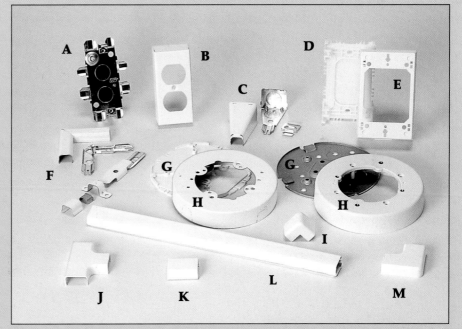

Typical raceway components: A–backing plate; **B**–receptacle coverplate; **C**–reducing converter and cover; **D**–tongued mounting plate; **E**–extension box; **F**–elbow connector and cover; **G**–fixture mounting plates; **H**–fixture extension boxes; **I**–90-deg. connector; **J**–T-connector cover; **K**–straight connector cover; **L**–channel; **M**–L-connector cover

Raceway Components

Raceway components are available in metal or plastic and must be joined mechanically and electrically to protect wires. Raceway fasteners must be flush with the channel surface so that they don't cut the wires. Raceways must be flame-retardant; resistant to moisture, impact, and crushing; and installed in a dry location.

chapter 3

wiring methods

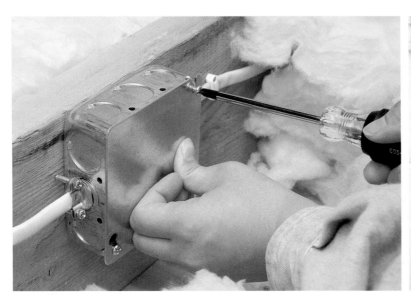

NOW THAT YOU'VE LEARNED the fundamentals of electricity and acquainted yourself with the tools, materials, and equipment that you may need to complete an electrical project, it's time to acquire some basic wiring skills. Before you begin any wiring project, however, remember that safety comes first. Working on a given circuit means first knowing to which breaker or fuse the circuit is connected. If it hasn't already been done, this is a good time for you to chart the circuits in your home. (See page 42.)

Basic Circuitry

Charting Circuits

Whether working with fuses or circuit breakers, you must know which switches, receptacles, fixtures, or equipment are on the circuits they control. You must also know how they work. There are many types of fuses and circuit breakers, each with its own function. The purpose of fuses and circuit breakers is to protect the wiring—not the appliance. Keep this in mind as you chart circuits, verifying that no fuse or circuit breaker has more amperage than the wire it is protecting. The maximum allowable current a

Fuse and Circuit Breaker Capacities

Fuse or Circuit Breaker		Wire Gauge Capacity	Load Capacity
15-Amp Fuse	15-Amp Circuit Breaker	14/2g	15 Amps
20-Amp Fuse	20-Amp Circuit Breaker	12/2g	20 Amps
30-Amp Fuse	30-Amp Circuit Breaker	10/2g	30 Amps

wire can carry, measured in amps, is called its *ampacity.*

While you are inspecting your fuse box or breaker panel, look for any obvious problems. For example, if you unscrew a fuse from a fuse box, examine both the fuse and its screw shell. (To be safe, first pull the main fuse.) Check the fuse or the screw shell for

any damage from arcing or burning.

Once you are certain that there is no damage to your fuse box or breaker panel, you may begin to chart your circuits. A plug-in radio will come in handy, as will an assistant, if you can find one. If necessary, you can do the work alone—it will just take a bit longer.

Overload Protection

The excessive current that is created by a short circuit, or by connecting equipment that overloads the circuit, can easily cause irreparable damage to electrical equipment. An electrical system must have some type of overload protection. This type of protection is provided by fuses and circuit breakers. (See "Service Panels," page 25.)

Ground-Fault Circuit Interrupters (GFCI)

Although a powerful current surging through a grounding system will melt (blow) a fuse or switch off (trip) a circuit breaker, a less powerful current may not. But such a current may be forceful enough to cause serious injury. The risk of this happening is especially great in moisture-prone locations, such as outdoors or in bathrooms. A ground-fault circuit interrupter, or GFCI, protects against this danger. If the amperage flowing through the black and white wires is equal, then the circuit is operating properly. But if the GFCI detects as little as a 0.005-amp difference between the two wires, then leakage is presumed and device breaks the circuit—rapidly enough to prevent a hazardous shock.

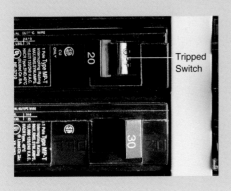

A circuit breaker switches off (trips) when the flow of current exceeds the breaker's capacity.

Tripped Switch

Charting Circuits

Identifying which circuits service all the receptacles, switches, lights, and appliances in your house takes some time. And it works best if you do it with a helper, so you'll have to draft someone for the afternoon and expel everyone else so things are quiet. The time and effort you spend on this job, however, are well worth it. By knowing which breaker controls which device, you can quickly turn off power to anything you are working on and avoid the risk of serious shock. Identifying the light and appliance circuits generally goes pretty fast. But checking all the receptacles can be time-consuming. Although they are usually grouped logically, there are bound to be circuits that combine receptacles from different rooms and, sometimes, different floors. Make sure to plug your radio or lamp into every receptacle in the house.

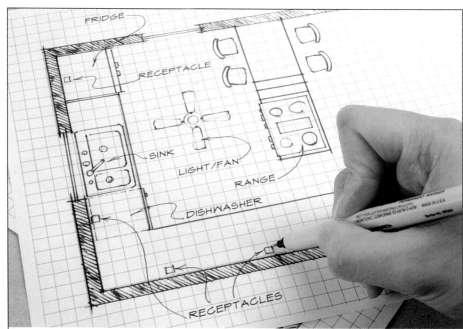

1 Before you label anything in your service panel box, make a scaled drawing of every room in your house. Draw the location of all the receptacles, light fixtures, switches, and appliances, and note where all the cabinets and furniture are positioned.

3 If you are working by yourself, adjust the radio to a high volume so that when you turn on the power you can hear from the service panel area if the radio comes on.

4 As you go from outlet to outlet, note on your room drawings which ones occupy which circuits. You'll need help to check if lights and ceiling fans turn on when you switch the breakers.

2 Once all the circuits are identified, go to the service panel and mark which breakers go to which circuits using stick-on labels. Then test each circuit by turning off the power, plugging in a radio (that's turned on) to any given outlet, and then turning the power on at the panel to see if the radio plays.

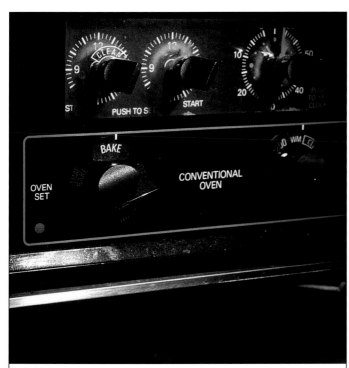

5 You will also need help from someone to check any appliance circuits. To do this with a range, for example, first turn off the breaker; then have a helper turn on the range. Next, turn on the breaker and see if the range comes on.

Checking for Damage

You can easily diagnose a blown fuse element by looking through the fuse glass. A burned element suggests an overload; a broken element and darkened glass suggests a short circuit.

When a plug fuse is blown, the fuse shell may also be damaged. Check it for signs of burning and arcing.

A damaged plug fuse will clearly show marks caused by burning and arcing.

Burn flashes in a circuit breaker panel are a telltale sign of serious damage.

Maximum Wires in a Box

Box Type and Size Electrical boxes must be of sufficient size to safely contain all enclosed wires. (Table 314.16(a), NEC)	Maximum Number of Wires Permitted						
	18 GA	16 GA	14 GA	12 GA	10 GA	8 GA	6 GA
4" x 1¼" Round or Octagonal	8	7	6	5	5	4	2
4" x 1½" Round or Octagonal	10	8	7	6	6	5	3
4" x 2⅛" Round or Octagonal	14	12	10	9	8	7	4
4" x 1¼" Square	12	10	9	8	7	6	3
4" x 1½" Square	14	12	10	9	8	7	4
4" x 2⅛" Square	20	17	15	13	12	10	6
3" x 2" x 2" Device Box	6	5	5	4	4	3	2
3" x 2" x 2½" Device Box	8	7	6	5	5	4	2
3" x 2" x 2¾" Device Box	9	8	7	6	5	4	2
3" x 2" x 3½" Device Box	12	10	9	8	7	6	3
4" x 2⅛" x 1½" Device Box	6	5	5	4	4	3	2
4" x 2⅛" x 1⅞" Device Box	8	7	6	5	5	4	2
4" x 2⅛" x 2⅛" Device Box	9	8	7	6	5	4	2
3¾" x 2" x 2½" Device Box	9	8	7	6	5	4	2
3¾" x 2" x 3½" Device Box	14	12	10	9	8	7	4

Calculating Ampacity

An overloaded circuit is a real danger in any electrical system and can easily lead to a blown fuse or tripped circuit breaker. Worse, it poses a potential fire hazard and can be a threat to both your life and property. The NEC requires that the demand on a given circuit be kept below its safe capacity (Section 220.14).

To calculate the total amperage of the circuit, add up those loads of which you know the amperage. For those loads that are listed in wattage instead of amperage, divide the wattage by the circuit voltage to get the amperage (amps = watts/volts), and add the values to the other amperage loads. Total amperage load for the circuit should not exceed the breaker or fuse rating.

This product label provides information about the amperage used by the device.

The safe capacity of a circuit equals only 80 percent of the maximum amp rating. For a typical 20-amp circuit, the circuit should carry just 16 amps. If you can't find the amperage or wattage of the appliance, use "Appliance Wattage," page 10.

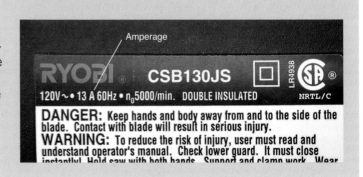

Basic Wiring

Height and Clearance Requirements

New-construction wiring proceeds from a power or lighting plan. Use these floor plans to lay out what is known as rough-in work. This includes installing the outlet boxes, running the wiring through the rough framing, stripping the wires inside the electrical boxes, and connecting the grounding wires. Because the electrical inspector will review the construction site and approve or reject the rough-in wiring, it is necessary to follow NEC requirements when installing wiring and electrical fixtures.

Clearance requirements are especially important to reduce the potential for fire hazards. For example, recessed fixtures not approved for contact with insulation must be spaced at least ½ inch from combustible materials (NEC Section 410.66). When locating receptacles and switches, adhere to specific height requirements both for reasons of safety and accessibility. Switches, for instance, are not permitted to be any higher than 6 feet 7 inches above the floor or working level (Section 404.8).

Installing Electrical Boxes

Both for ease of use and aesthetics, receptacle and switch boxes should be kept at a uniform height above the finished floor or work surface. A general rule of thumb is to center receptacle boxes 12 inches above the floor—18 inches for handicapped accessibility. Center receptacle boxes over countertops 4 feet above the finished floor, as well as receptacle boxes in bathrooms and garages. Laundry receptacles are placed at a height of 3½ feet. Switch boxes, on the other hand, are normally centered 4 feet above the finished floor—the maximum for handicapped accessibility.

A common type of electrical box used in residential work today is a nonmetallic (plastic or fiberglass) box that may include integral nails for fastening it to stud framing. Nonmetallic boxes such as this are inexpensive and easy to install. You place the box against a stud, bring the face of the box flush to where the drywall will be after it is installed, and then nail the box in place. Be sure to purchase boxes that have enough depth—at least 1¼ to 1½ inches. This will give you approximately 23 cubic inches of interior box volume in which to tuck your wires. Using cable staples, secure the nonmetallic cable no more than 12 inches from the single-device electrical box. Make sure that at least ¼ inch of fully insulated cable will be secured inside of the box after the wires are stripped. Many switch boxes have gauge marks on their sides that allow you to position the box on a framing stud without having to measure depth. Recess boxes no more than ¼ inch from the finished wall surface. Mount boxes flush with the surface of combustible materials, such as wood.

Another type of electrical box is the handy box: a single-switch/receptacle box that is often screwed directly to a framing member, using a portable electric drill with a screwdriver bit. They sometimes come with a side-mounting flange to aid in installation. One danger, however, is that most handy boxes do not have adequate depth and can, therefore, only accommodate one cable safely. Misuse of this type of box is a code violation and should be avoided.

On masonry surfaces, attach boxes using masonry anchors and screws. Simply drill anchor holes in the masonry; then insert the anchors, and mount the box.

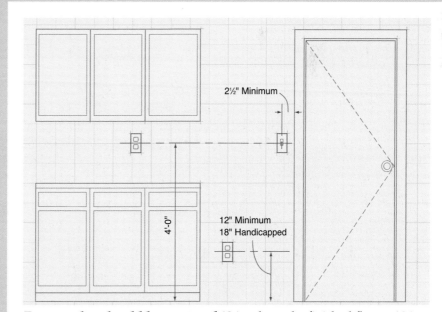

Receptacles should be centered 12 in. above the finished floor—18 in. for handicapped accessibility. Receptacles over countertops should be centered 4 ft. above the finished floor. Switches are generally centered at this same height, which is the maximum for handicapped accessibility.

Stripping Wires and Cables

There are many different ways to strip electrical cable, but probably the easiest is to use a combination of a cable ripper to peel off the plastic sheathing, followed by a multipurpose tool or wire strippers to remove the insulation on the wires. Most boxes require that about 8 inches of cable wire extend into the box. So strip off 8 inches of sheathing first; then take off about ⅝ inch of insulation from the end of each wire. Slide this cable into the box, and attach the outlet device.

1 To remove the plastic sheathing from an electrical cable, use a cable ripper. Slide this simple tool over the end of the cable; then squeeze the halves together to pierce the sheathing (top). To cut the sheathing, pull the ripper to the end of the cable (above).

PRO TIP

If you have a lot of wiring to do, it may be worth investing in an automatic wire stripper. To use it, just feed the end of the wire into the stripper and squeeze. It cuts the wire insulation to the proper length and depth and pulls the cut insulation off the wire.

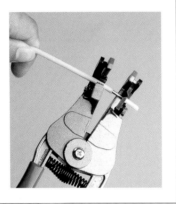

2 Once the sheathing is cut to the end of the cable, pull back the sheathing to where the cable was first pierced (top), and cut off the sheathing using a multipurpose tool or a utility knife at this point (bottom).

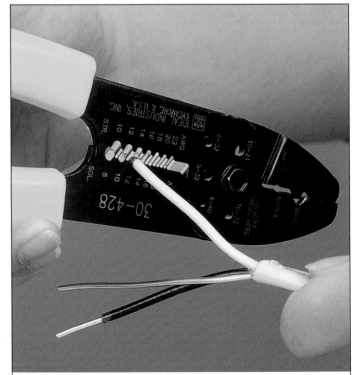

3 Use a multipurpose tool to strip the insulation from the ends of the wire. Take off about ⅝ in. of insulation, using the appropriate slot on the tool that matches the gauge of the wire.

Preparing for Inspection

Once new framing walls are ready to be wired and electrical boxes have all been put in place, carefully begin pulling the cable through the framing. (See below and pages 48–49.) When you insert a cable end into an electrical box, leave a minimum of 8 inches of extra cable, cutting away the excess. Using a cable staple, secure the cable at a maximum of 8 inches above the single-device box. After you have run all cables through the framing and into the electrical boxes, rip back and remove the sheathing from the cable ends in each box; then strip the individual wires. Before a rough-in inspection can be done, you must also splice together the grounding wires using either green

wire connectors (bottom) or wire crimping ferrules. Then place the wires securely in their boxes.

After a rough-in inspection is performed, install the receptacles and switches. Wait until the drywall is in place before doing this work. When the walls are completed and all of the boxes wired, you can install cover plates and turn on the power. Check each receptacle, using a plug-in receptacle analyzer, to verify that all of the wiring has been properly done. Install the light fixtures; then confirm that they are all working. Once you have completed all of this, your work will be ready for final inspection. The inspector will reexamine your work, performing many of the same circuit tests as you.

Attic and Crawl Space Runs

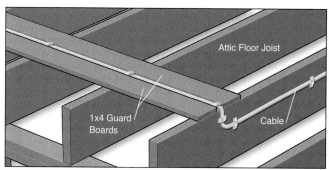

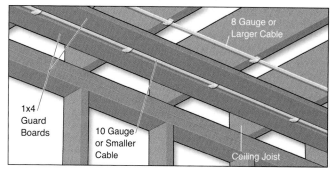

Attic Runs. To run cable perpendicular to framing joists in an unfinished attic, construct a channel space along an edge wall, using two 1x4 furring strips as guard boards, as shown. You can also drill holes through the middle of the joists and run the cable through these holes. This option is a poor choice if insulation is in the way.

Crawl Space Runs. To run cable perpendicular to framing joists in an unfinished basement or crawl space, construct a runway using a 1x4 furring strip along the bottom edge of the framing or bore holes in the joists. You can staple cable containing three 8-gauge conductors or larger directly to the underside of the joists.

PRO TIP

Splicing Grounding Wires

In existing wiring you're likely to come across the pigtail method of splicing grounding wires (in the photo at right), so that's the method demonstrated throughout this book. However, grounding wire connectors are manufactured with a hole at the top so that wires can be spliced as shown at far right. This is the method actually preferred by electricians these days.

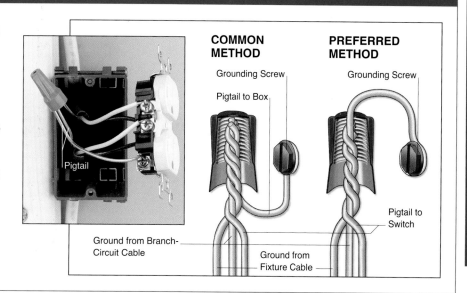

Running Cable through Framing

Installing wiring through new construction is relatively easy. The most common electrical installations are those in which outlet boxes are mounted alongside a stud or joist, although this is not always possible. Once electrical boxes are in place, run the cable through the framing members. Do this by drilling ¾-inch holes directly through the center of the studs or joists. Center the holes at least 1⅝ inches in from the edge of the framing member. If you must drill closer, then attach a wire shield to the outer edge of the framing to prevent nails or screws from penetrating the hole and causing damage to the cable during the course of future work.

If you cannot drill holes through framing because the framing cavity contains ductwork or plumbing, you may have to resort to surface wiring to do the job properly. (See "Surface Wiring," page 57.)

Avoiding Damage. Be careful not to jerk the wire cable violently as you pull it through the drilled holes in the framing. The friction from pulling cable through rough-cut wood can cause the cable sheathing to tear, exposing the wires to serious damage. You should also avoid making sharp bends or kinks in the cable, as these too can damage the wiring. In addition, be careful when running cable along the bottom of a wall—there are likely to be toenailed fasteners near the bottom of each wall stud.

Getting around windows and doors can also be a problem. If there are cripple studs above the header, then you can drill holes through them for cable. However, you can't drill through the length of a solid-wood header. If possible, you can go over or under such obstacles. As a last resort, use a router to cut a

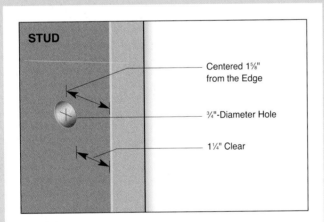

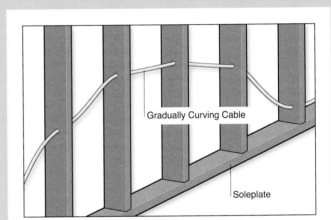

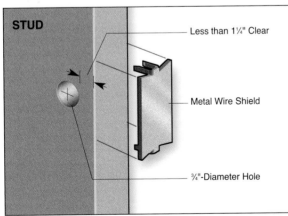

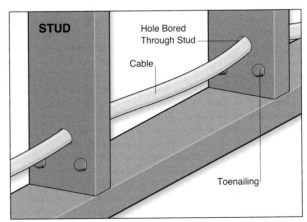

A bored hole must clear the edge of a framing stud by at least 1¼ in. A ¾-in. hole, for example, must be centered at least 1⅝ in. in from the outer edge of a wall stud. If the hole edge is closer to the stud edge than this, it must be protected by a metal wire shield (NEC Section 300.4).

Allow the cable to sag or curve slightly, rather than pulling it tightly through a stud wall, to prevent potential kinks, sharp bends, or overstretching of the wire. When drilling holes near the soleplate of a stud-framed wall, steer clear of toenailing and other metal fasteners that may snag your drill bit.

channel deeply enough across the surface of the header to accommodate a cable; protect the cable by installing metal plates over it.

Holes and Notches. If you bore holes through ceiling and floor joists, the holes must be located so that they will not undermine the structural integrity of the framing. (See illustration below.) This is also a concern if you notch the wood along the top or bottom edge to run cable perpendicular to the joists. In this instance, you must install metal wire shields to protect the cable from damage. Even cable that runs parallel with framing should not be left vulnerable or hanging loosely in a wall or floor space. Use cable staples to secure it in place along the center of the stud, joist, or rafter.

Cripple studs, left, over a header offer a simple and convenient path for wiring around a door or window opening. The best way to go around a solid header, right, is to run your wiring through the ceiling joists above or the floor joists below the rough opening.

HOLES & NOTCHES

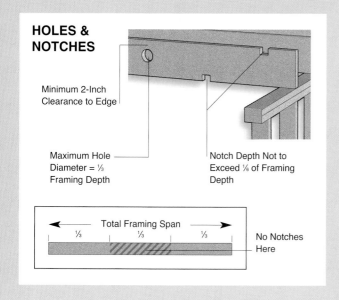

Minimum 2-Inch Clearance to Edge

Maximum Hole Diameter = ⅓ Framing Depth

Notch Depth Not to Exceed ⅙ of Framing Depth

Total Framing Span
⅓   ⅓   ⅓

No Notches Here

Routing a Solid Header

Use a router to cut a minimum ⅝ x ⅜-in. cable channel across a solid header only if you have no other alternative. Attach a series of metal plates (shown as cutaway, bottom) over the routed cable channel to protect the cable from potential nail damage.

Channel Cut by Router

Channel Cut by Router   Metal Plate

Fishing Cable from below the Floor

Fishing cable through closed walls can be difficult. Here are some tips to make it easier: always use a cut-in box for the outlet; use a guide wire to establish one reference point for two different floors; be willing to waste some wire by running the cable into the basement and then to its destination, rather than taking the shorter, but usually much harder, route through the wall.

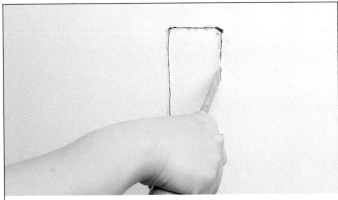

1 Trace the outline of a cut-in box on the wall, and cut along this line using a drywall or keyhole saw.

2 Drill a small hole through the floor directly below this box opening in the wall.

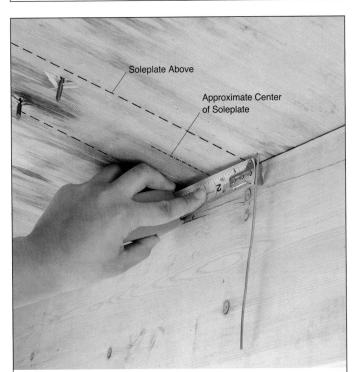

Soleplate Above

Approximate Center of Soleplate

4 Estimate that the middle of the wall's sole plate is about 2 in. away from the guide wire. Mark this centerline along the bottom surface of the floor plywood.

Soleplate Above

5 Using a drill with a ¾-in. spade bit, bore a hole up through the plywood and wall plate. Unwind some cable from the roll, and push the free end up through this hole. Be sure to push up enough cable to reach the box hole. Tape the cable in place so it doesn't fall out.

Soleplate Above

½" ±

3 Use a piece of scrap wire as a guide to locate the hole under the floor. Because the hole was drilled right next to the wall, the wall framing should begin about ½ in. away from the guide wire.

6 If you can fit your hand into the box hole, reach in and grab the cable. If not, get some help from someone with smaller hands. Once you pull the cable out, install it in a cut-in box; then push the box into the wall, and secure it in place.

Opening and Closing Walls

Running cables through existing walls and joist spaces is a lot more complicated than running cables in new construction. Because you cannot see into finished framing cavities, fishing cables through walls and ceilings requires great patience and more than a little skill.

If you have access to walls from a basement or attic, you can get power into walls by fishing the cable vertically instead of horizontally through the structural framing. In many cases, running cable the long way around to complete a circuit may be the easiest route, even if you have to spend more money for cable. The cost of the cable is likely to be much less than that of ripping into walls and ceilings. If you must run cable across existing framing, for example, you may have to cut into drywall in order to position the cable properly. It is a good idea to take time initially to explore alternative routes the cable might follow. Try to determine the best route; then make a rough sketch or map of the cable route. This will undoubtedly save you time and money later.

Before running cable, first decide where to locate your new switch, outlet, or junction box; then determine which walls or ceilings, if any, need to be opened to efficiently route the cable to this point. You can cut openings in drywall using a utility knife, mini-hacksaw, or keyhole or saber saw. After you make your cut, either remove the scrap or knock it back between the framing members.

In an unfinished basement, you may encounter hollow concrete-block walls or poured steel-reinforced solid concrete walls. Although it is possible to cut into a hollow concrete-block wall, it isn't practical. For block and concrete walls, it is best to install metal surface raceways or electrical conduit, and surface-mount your electrical boxes and wiring. Use a masonry bit on your power drill to make pilot holes for masonry anchors; then anchor the boxes and conduit clamps directly to the wall.

A   A

B   C

Flat square electrical boxes are specially made to fit in shallow furred-out wall cavities. **A**–shallow boxes; **B**–box extension; **C**–box cover

Running Cable behind a Baseboard

One of the best ways to run new cable in a finished room is to remove the baseboard and install the cable in the stud space. The job isn't very hard, and you can make it even easier by being careful when you remove the baseboard. Reuse the old baseboard to save some money, but more importantly, you can save a lot of time and effort. If you are installing a thinner, low-voltage cable for such things as a telephone, TV, or doorbell, you may be able to save a lot of work if your baseboard has a shoe molding at the bottom. Often, when you remove the shoe, there will be enough space to tuck small cables below the base and behind the shoe. If the wire does fit, just make sure to nail the shoe to the baseboard, not the floor, when you replace it. This will keep the nails away from the cable.

1 Installing cable behind a baseboard is one of the best ways to route cable through existing walls. The first step is to mark the wall along the top of the baseboard (left). Then cut along the joint between the baseboard and the wall to break the seal made by caulk and paint (right).

4 Use a utility knife or a keyhole saw to cut through the drywall along the cut line. Once the piece is free, pull it away from the wall. If the drywall was screwed in place, remove the screws so the piece of drywall comes out cleanly and can be reused.

5 The cable can run either in notches cut in the edge of the studs, as shown here, or in holes drilled through the middle of the studs. If you notch the studs, install a metal shield on each stud to protect the cable.

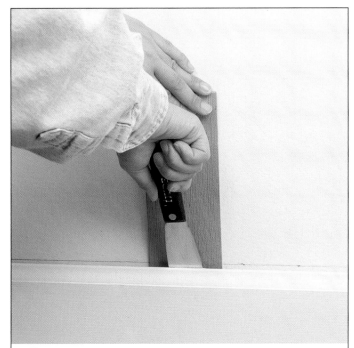

2 Carefully pry off the baseboard using a putty knife and a shimming shingle. Work the knife blade between the two, and pry them apart enough to slide the shingle behind the knife. The shingle protects the wall surface from damage.

3 Measure down from the wall reference line ½ in., and mark the wall every couple of feet. Using a long straightedge and pencil, draw a cut line through these marks.

6 Once the cable is entirely installed, cover up the opening with the piece of drywall you removed, if it's still useable, or with a new piece. Drive the nails or screws in the studs and bottom plate to avoid hitting the metal shields.

7 Reinstall the old baseboard, or cut and install a new baseboard that matches the other trim in the room. Then caulk the joint between the baseboard and the wall, and paint the joint and the baseboard.

3 Wiring Methods

Fishing Cable across a Ceiling

Running cable through an existing, but inaccessible, ceiling may require that you cut both a ceiling and a wall opening in order to fish the cable from a vertical wall cavity to a horizontal ceiling cavity. Once the ceiling is opened, use a fish tape to get the cable across to the new electrical box.

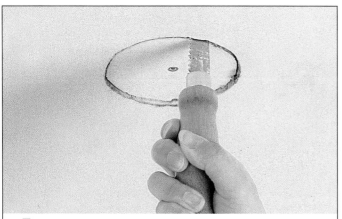

1 Determine where you want your ceiling outlet; then trace around the fixture box. Using a drywall or keyhole saw, cut along the line and remove the drywall.

2 Measure from the end wall of the room to the ceiling hole. Then go to the side room wall and transfer this measurement to the corner between the wall and ceiling.

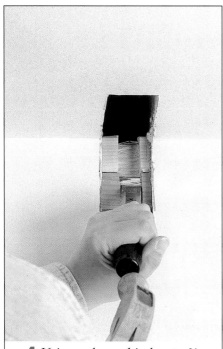

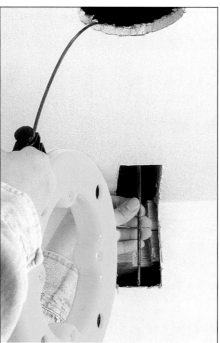

4 Using a sharp chisel, cut a ¾-in.-wide by 1-in.-deep notch in the wall plates. This notch will act as a raceway for the electrical cable that will service the ceiling fixture.

5 Use a fish tape to pull cable into the box. Start by feeding the tape into the ceiling hole, directing it through the access hole in the ceiling and down to the box hole near the floor.

6 Tape the end of some electrical cable to the end of the fish tape, and pull the cable up through the box hole at the floor.

3 Measure down from the wall reference line ½ in., and mark the wall every couple of feet. Using a long straightedge and pencil, draw a cut line through these marks.

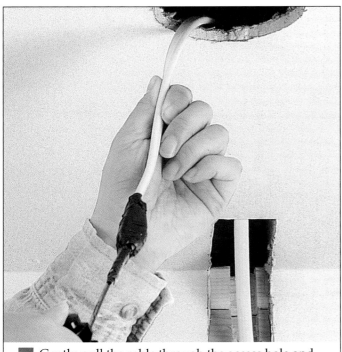

7 Gently pull the cable through the access hole and the outlet hole in the ceiling. Cover the cable at the top plates notch with a metal shield.

Wiring around an Existing Doorway

If an existing doorway is in the path of your cable, you will have to run the cable up and around the door frame. In this situation, rather than cutting out sections of the drywall, you may be able to take advantage of the shim space. Remove the molding from around the door, gently prying it away from the wall. Use a rigid paint scraper with a scrap piece of wood under it to protect the wall. If you cannot remove the trim without causing it damage, you may have to replace the molding. If the molding is irreplaceable, you may wish to reconsider using this method to route the cable around your door. Once the shim space is exposed, notch out the shim spacers just enough to accommodate the cable. String the cable around the shim space; then cover the notched areas, using metal wire shields. When you replace the casing molding, be sure to nail it to the doorjambs only in the places that are protected by the metal shields. Keep in mind that these shims will keep the casing from sitting flush against the jambs, even after the boards are nailed in place. To fix this, just fill the gaps with latex caulk, let it dry for a while, then prime and paint the caulk and the casing the same color.

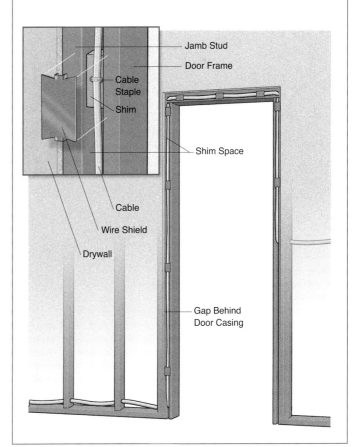

Jamb Stud
Door Frame
Cable Staple
Shim
Shim Space
Cable
Wire Shield
Drywall
Gap Behind Door Casing

3 Wiring Methods

Fixing a Spliced Circuit using a Junction Box

No wire splices outside an electrical box are permitted by the NEC. But this doesn't mean that they don't occur, particularly in old houses that have suffered at the hands of sloppy or uninformed electricians. If you have any of these splices in your house, you must take apart the existing splice; install a junction box; make the new splices using wire connectors; and cover the box with a protective metal cover plate. That way the wire-to-wire connections are secure and protected from possible damage. Fortunately, you can find a junction box for just about any location and there are box extensions in case you need to make the box deeper. Separate cable clamps that you slide into the holes created by the knockouts protect the cable from chafing against the sharp edges of the box.

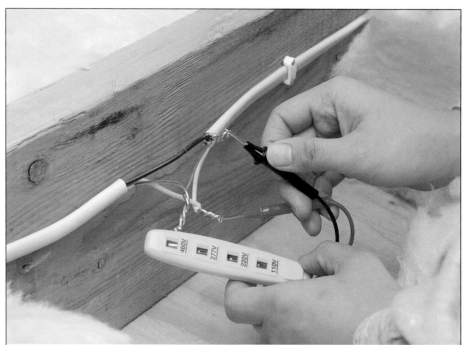

1 Turn off the power to the circuit with the splice in the cable. Remove any wire connectors or electrical tape from the wires. Then check for any power with a neon circuit tester. If you find power, immediately locate the proper circuit breaker and turn it off.

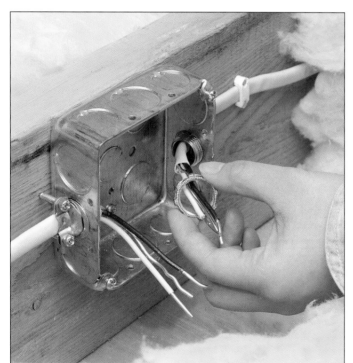

3 Put cable connectors into both knockout openings; then slide the cables through the connectors; and tighten the cable clamps onto the cable. Finish up by turning the locknuts onto the connectors from inside the box. Secure these nuts using slip joint pliers.

4 Splice all the like-colored wires in the box using the proper wire connectors for the wire gauge in the cable. Red-colored connectors usually work for both two 14-gauge wires and two 12-gauge wires. Green connectors are used for ground wires.

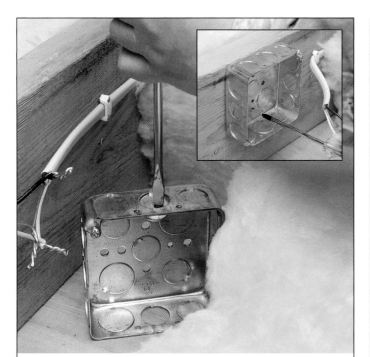

2 For the wires to have access to the junction box, remove a couple of knockout plates using a screwdriver and a hammer. Then separate the splices, and install the box so it falls midway between the ends of both cables. Screw or nail the box in place (inset).

5 Carefully push all the spliced wires into the junction box, and install the box cover plate. Turn on the circuit power at the breaker panel, and check to see if all the receptacles, switches, and lights on the circuit are working properly.

Surface Wiring

Conditions exist where concealed wiring isn't possible—for example, a basement having exposed concrete or masonry walls. In this case, surface wiring is the only option. Surface-mounted conduit, or raceway, provides a rigid flat metal or plastic pipe to convey wire across instead of inside a wall or ceiling. Special receptacle and fixture boxes are used in conjunction with raceway to offer a safe way to install surface wiring. A plastic raceway requires the inclusion of a separate grounding wire; a metal raceway connected to a properly wired and grounded electrical box is self-grounding.

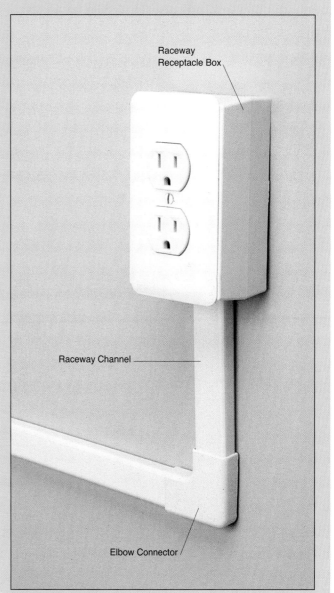

Raceway channels protect exposed wire along a wall or ceiling surface.

Adding a New Circuit

Remodeling plans often call for adding new electrical circuits to meet increased demands. In addition, appliances such as dishwashers and waste-disposal units often require a separate circuit to power the appliance. You will need to run wiring from the appliance to the main panel. Working on a service panel is dangerous, so take all safety measures. If your installation is special in any way or if you are not confident of completing the hookup correctly, have a licensed electrician do the work at the panel after you have done the room wiring. Many local building codes require that a licensed electrician make the final hookups at the panel anyway.

Start by turning off the power at the top of the service panel. Then bring your new circuit cable into the box by removing one of the knockout plates at the side or bottom of the box. Install a cable connecter, and tighten it against the wire and against the box. Strip about ⅝ inch of insulation off the ends of the black and white wires; then install the white and ground wires in the neutral/grounding bus bar. Install the black wire in the end of a breaker.

If you need to add a breaker for a 240-volt circuit, get a special breaker that occupies two slots in the panel box. The cable will have two hot wires—one black and one red. Insert one of the hot wires into each of two holes in the double breaker.

1 Open the door to the panel box, and turn off the main breaker switch, usually at the top of the box. Remove the panel cover by backing out the screws at the corners.

4 To attach a cable to the panel box, first remove a knockout plate from the side of the box. Then install a cable connector in this hole by threading a locknut on the inside end of the connector. Slide the cable through the connecter, and tighten the cable-clamp screws.

Cable Clamp

Locknut

5 Once the cable clamps are tight, return to the locknut and tighten it securely. Do this by holding the blade of a flat-blade screwdriver against one of the locknut ridges and driving it in a clockwise direction using a hammer.

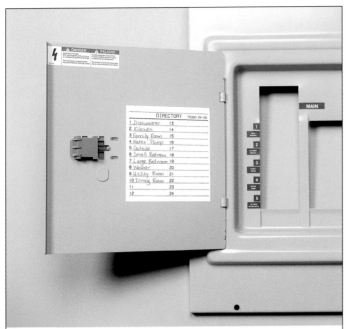

2 Note the circuit identification list. This list should reference every circuit that is wired into the panel.

Main Breaker

Spare Breaker

3 When you add a new circuit, you have to add a new circuit breaker to protect it. Check your panel box to see if you have room for another breaker, or if you have a breaker installed that's not being used (see above). You can tell it's not being used because no black wire is attached to it.

Neutral/ Grounding Bus

Hot Bus

Setscrew

6 In most service panels, there are two bus bars for attaching the neutral and ground wires. Both bars can take both colored wires but only one wire should be put into each hole. The black circuit wire goes under the setscrew on the breaker (inset).

MAIN

7 If you added a new breaker to the panel, then remove the knockout on the panel cover. If you are using a spare breaker, the knockout is already gone and you can just put the cover back on. Record the new circuit on the panel door, and turn on the main breaker.

receptacles & switches

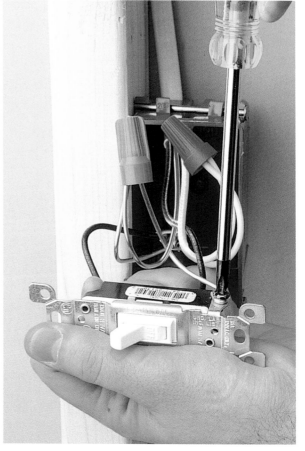

Receptacles

Duplex Receptacles

Although there are two basic types of receptacles—single and duplex—only duplex receptacles are commonly found in modern homes. A duplex receptacle accommodates two plugs at the same time. Originally, receptacles were neither grounded nor polarized; later, they became polarized but not grounded. Today, receptacles include a screw terminal for a grounding connection. These receptacles have a total of five terminal screws: two brass screw terminals on the right side for black/red hot-wire connections; two silver screw terminals on the left side for white neutral-wire connections; and one green screw terminal on the left side for a bare copper or green grounding-wire connection. How many wires are connected to a receptacle is determined by whether the connection occurs at the end or in the middle of a wiring run. An end-of-run receptacle will have only one cable entering the box, while a middle-of-run receptacle will have two.

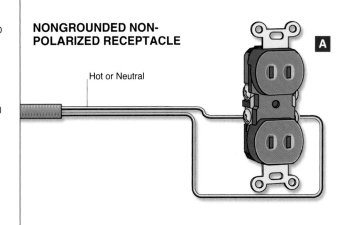

NONGROUNDED NON-POLARIZED RECEPTACLE

Hot or Neutral

A

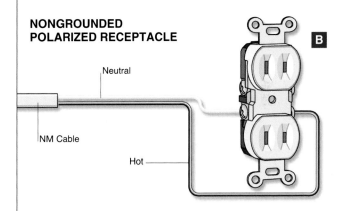

NONGROUNDED POLARIZED RECEPTACLE

Neutral

NM Cable

Hot

B

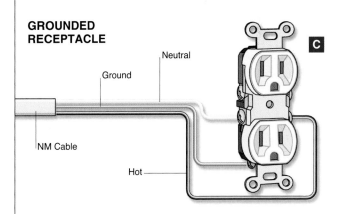

GROUNDED RECEPTACLE

Ground

Neutral

NM Cable

Hot

C

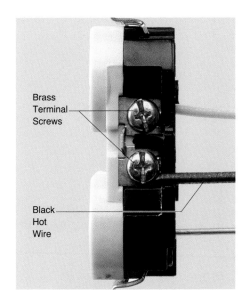

White Neutral Wire

Silver Terminal Screws

Grounding Wire

Grounding Terminal Screw

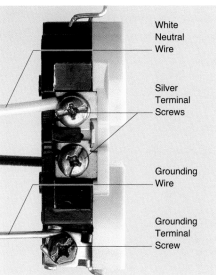

Brass Terminal Screws

Black Hot Wire

Receptacle, right side. The hot black or red wires are connected to the brass terminal screws on a receptacle.

Receptacle, left side. The silver terminal screws on a receptacle receive the white neutral wires, while the green terminal screw receives the grounding wire.

Receptacle History

Early receptacles had two nonpolarized connections **(A)**. For this type of receptacle, the colored wires could go to either screw terminal. Later, manufacturers made polarized receptacles **(B)**. These require that a specific color wire be connected to a specific screw terminal, but they are not grounded. Today, receptacles also include a green grounding screw terminal **(C)**.

Sequential 120-Volt Duplex Receptacles

Start- or middle-of-run receptacles are connected to all wires from both directions. End-of-run receptacles are the last on the circuit and have only two terminations and a ground connection.

Multiple 120-Volt Duplex Receptacle Circuit

On multiple 120-volt receptacle circuits, three-wire cable is used to connect all but the last receptacle. The white neutral wire is shared by both circuits.

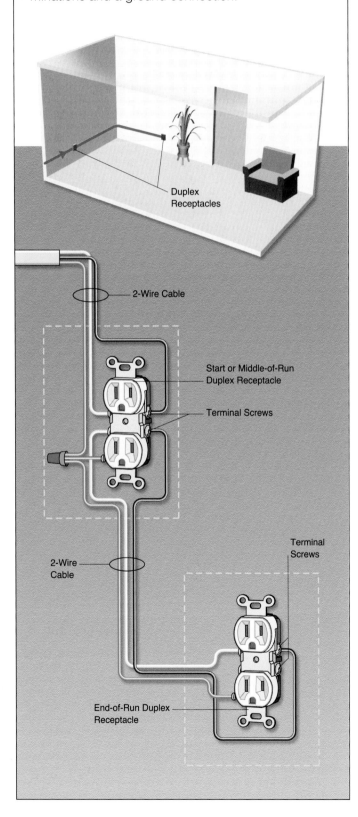

Duplex Receptacles

2-Wire Cable

Start or Middle-of-Run Duplex Receptacle

Terminal Screws

2-Wire Cable

Terminal Screws

End-of-Run Duplex Receptacle

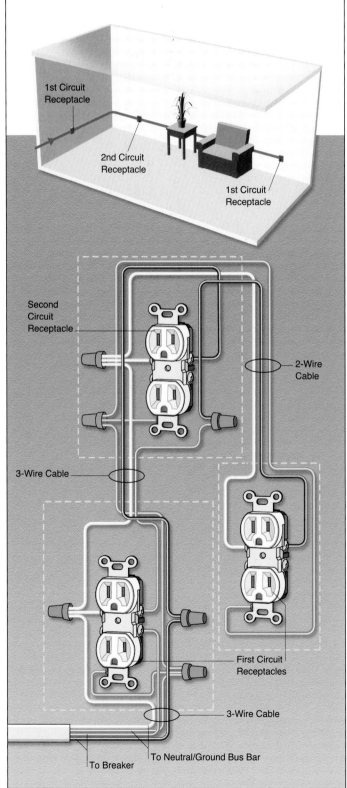

1st Circuit Receptacle

2nd Circuit Receptacle

1st Circuit Receptacle

Second Circuit Receptacle

2-Wire Cable

3-Wire Cable

First Circuit Receptacles

3-Wire Cable

To Breaker

To Neutral/Ground Bus Bar

Wiring a Split-Circuit Receptacle

The metal tabs connecting the screw terminals on each side of a receptacle can be removed. By breaking the connection between the brass screw terminals you can wire the top outlet of the receptacle independently from the bottom. The silver tabs are normally left intact. This permits two appliances in a single receptacle to be powered by different circuits.

CODE TIP

Tamper-Proof Receptacles

The NEC® requires that 15- and 20-amp receptacles in new construction be listed as tamper-proof. This code change is designed to keep a child from inserting an object into one of the contact slots. One company has produced receptacles that look like standard units, but they contain, inside the receptacle, plastic shields that spring into place when a plug is removed. Inserting an object into one of the slots will not dislodge the shields. The only way to move the shield is to depress the shields simultaneously, as when inserting a plug into the contact slots. Check with your local building department for exact requirements.

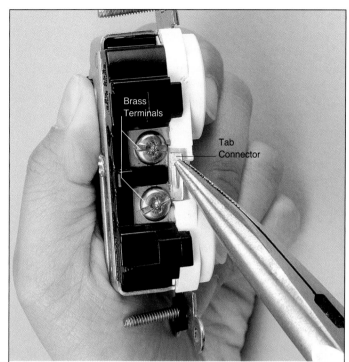

1 Remove the tab connector between the brass terminal screws by breaking it away with long-nose pliers. This allows you to wire outlets on a duplex receptacle independently.

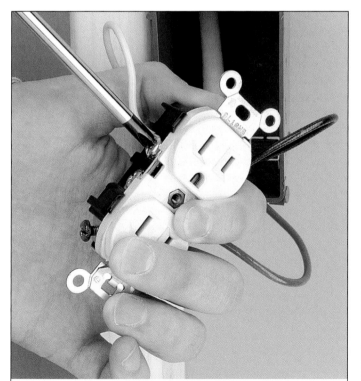

2 Once the tab has been removed, attach the two hot wires to the brass terminal screws. Don't remove the tab that joins the silver screws. Just attach the white (neutral) wire to either silver screw.

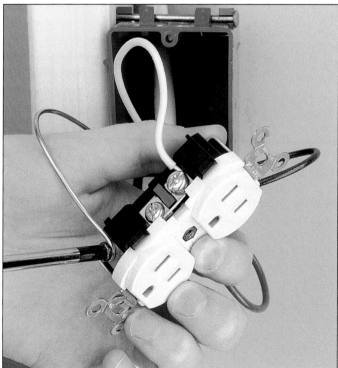

3 Attach the grounding wire to the grounding screw on the receptacle. Then push the receptacle into the box; attach it with screws; and install a cover plate.

Wiring a Switch/Receptacle

Combine a grounded receptacle with a single-pole switch to make up for a lack of receptacles in a room. You can wire a switch/receptacle combination in one of two ways—either the switch controls the receptacle or, more commonly, the receptacle remains constantly active while the switch powers a separate fixture. This type of circuit must occur in the middle of a run.

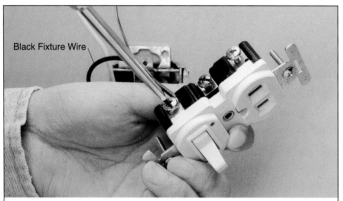

Black Fixture Wire

1 Connect the black fixture wire to the brass screw on the side of the switch unit

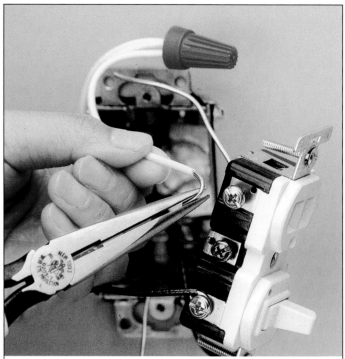

2 Attach the black power wire to the terminal screw on the other side of the switch. Join the white neutral wires with a white pigtail, and attach the other end of the pigtail to the silver receptacle screw.

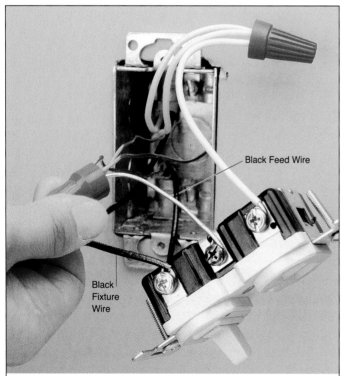

Black Feed Wire

Black Fixture Wire

3 Join the ground wires and two pigtail grounds with a wire connector. One pigtail is attached to the grounding screw in the metal box. The other is attached to the grounding screw on the side of the switch/receptacle.

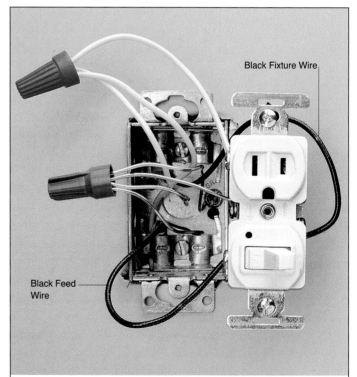

Black Fixture Wire

Black Feed Wire

4 If you want to control the receptacle with the switch, instead of controlling another device, such as a light fixture, then just switch the locations of the black wires as shown above.

Single-Pole Switch with Light Fixture and Duplex Receptacle

Wire a middle-of-run light fixture through a single-pole switch using two-wire cable to power the switch and three-wire cable from the switch to the fixture. Continue the circuit to an end-of-run receptacle using two-wire cable.

Split Receptacle Controlled by End-of-Run Switch

In this configuration, one-half of a split receptacle (tab removed) is powered by a switch located at the end of the circuit run. The other half of the receptacle is constantly powered. Mark the white neutral wire with black tape to indicate that it is hot.

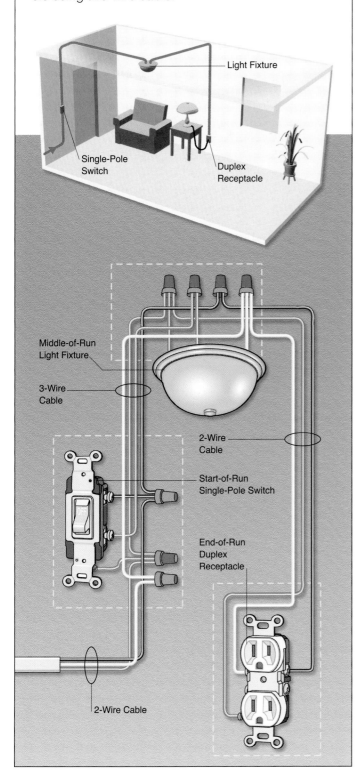

Light Fixture

Single-Pole Switch

Duplex Receptacle

Middle-of-Run Light Fixture

3-Wire Cable

2-Wire Cable

Start-of-Run Single-Pole Switch

End-of-Run Duplex Receptacle

2-Wire Cable

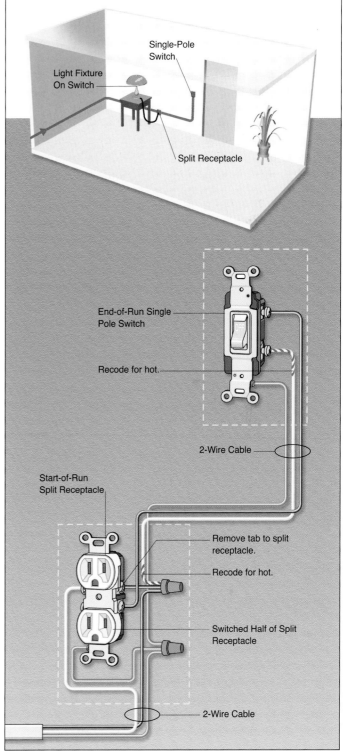

Single-Pole Switch

Light Fixture On Switch

Split Receptacle

End-of-Run Single Pole Switch

Recode for hot.

2-Wire Cable

Start-of-Run Split Receptacle

Remove tab to split receptacle.

Recode for hot.

Switched Half of Split Receptacle

2-Wire Cable

Duplex Receptacle with Split Receptacle Controlled by Start-of-Run Switch

To install a split receptacle controlled by a switch, remove the tab on the receptacle. Using two-wire cable, connect the switch to the power source. One hot wire from the switch connects to each half of the receptacle.

Duplex Receptacle with Split Receptacle Controlled by End-of-Run Switch

In this combination, the split receptacle is located at the start of the cable run. One-half of the receptacle is controlled by the switch. The other half of the receptacle is always hot and feeds the remainder of the circuit.

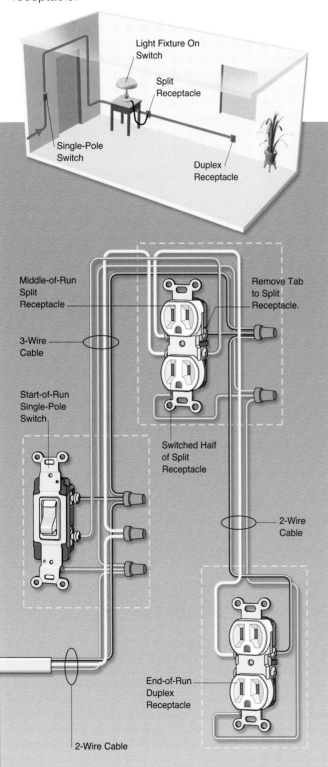

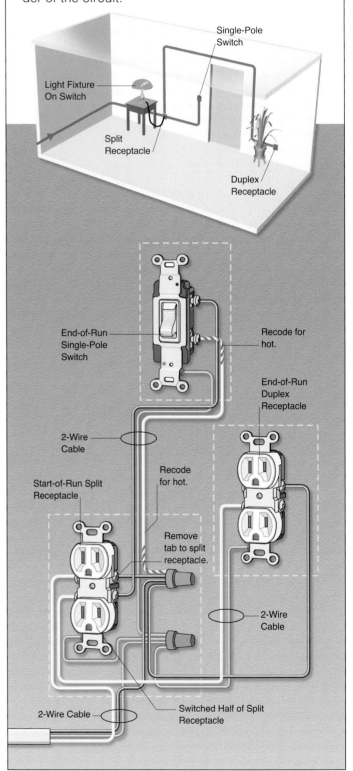

Interpreting a Receptacle

The labels or markings that appear on a receptacle convey important information about safety and usage. A UL label, for instance, means that the device has been certified for safety by the American Underwriters Laboratories, while a CSA label indicates approval by the Canadian equivalent—the Canadian Standards Association. Also shown are amperage and voltage ratings, which state the maximum permitted for the device. You should be especially alert to the acceptable wire usage designation, which indicates what kind of wire is safe to connect to the receptacle. A CU label means that only copper wire can be used; CO/ALR indicates that aluminum wires are acceptable; and CU/AL specifies copper or copper-clad aluminum wires only.

The screw terminal colors on a receptacle also denote specific information. Use the brass screw terminals for black/red hot wires, the silver screw terminals for white neutral wires, and the green terminal screw for the grounding connection.

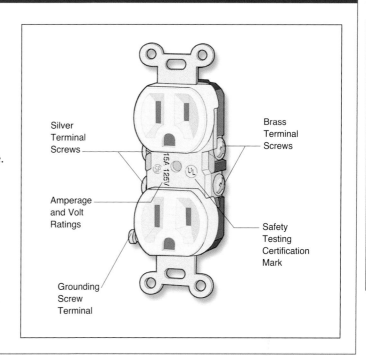

Silver Terminal Screws

Brass Terminal Screws

Amperage and Volt Ratings

Safety Testing Certification Mark

Grounding Screw Terminal

High-Voltage Receptacles

Large appliances in a home often draw significantly more current than smaller appliances. For this reason, contemporary homes usually have two types of receptacles—one type provides low-voltage power (120 volts), and the other provides high-voltage power (240 volts). Appliances that are rated for 240 volts—such as cooking ranges, clothes dryers, and air conditioners—are required to be connected to a single circuit. Most high-voltage appliances are connected to either a flush- or surface-mounted receptacle box. A nonmetallic sheathed cable containing two hot wires, each carrying 120 volts, and a grounding wire typically form an end-of-run connection within the receptacle box, which must be located within the length of the appliance cord. Because no neutral wire is needed, the white wire is coded, using black tape, to indicate that it is hot. However, a high-voltage circuit that also requires 120-volt current to operate clocks, timers, and lights does need to have a white neutral wire connected to the receptacle—so that the appliance can split the entering current between 120 volts and 240 volts. These circuits use three-wire cable.

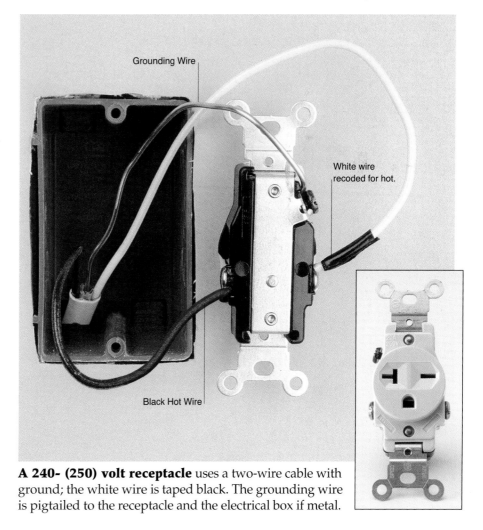

Grounding Wire

White wire recoded for hot.

Black Hot Wire

A 240- (250) volt receptacle uses a two-wire cable with ground; the white wire is taped black. The grounding wire is pigtailed to the receptacle and the electrical box if metal.

GFCI Receptacles

A ground-fault circuit interrupter (GFCI) is an electrical device that prevents electrocution caused by an accident or equipment malfunction. In a general-purpose, 120-volt household circuit, current moves along two insulated wires—one white and one black. Power is brought to the device or appliance by the black wire and returns from it by the white wire. As long as these two current flows remain equal, then the circuit operates normally and safely. However, if a portion of the return current is missing, or "faulted," a GFCI will immediately open the circuit in $\frac{1}{25}$th to $\frac{1}{30}$th of a second—25 to 30 times faster than a heartbeat. In this fraction of a second, you may receive a jolt of a shock, rather than the dangerous or potentially lethal shock that would otherwise occur in a circuit without the protection of a ground-fault circuit interrupter.

A GFCI receptacle, however, is not foolproof. For a ground-fault circuit interrupter to succeed, a ground-fault must first occur. This happens when current flows out of the normal circuit to a ground pathway, causing the imbalance between the black and white wires mentioned earlier. In this instance, if you place your body between the black and white wires, and you are not grounded, the GFCI will not function properly because it has no way of distinguishing your body from any other current-drawing device. The number of electrons entering the circuit is equal to the number of electrons returning from the circuit, except that they are passing first through the resistance within your body—causing your heart to go into fibrillation, beating erratically. If your heartbeat is not quickly restored to normal, then you will die. Even if the circuit is connected to a breaker panel, the breaker will not trip unless the internal current exceeds 15 or 20 amps—2,500 times more than is necessary to cause electrocution. A breaker or fuse is only designed to protect your household wiring against excessive current—it is not designed to protect you.

Required GFCI Locations. Even though GFCI circuits are not foolproof, they are nevertheless required in certain locations within a dwelling unit. These locations include, but are not strictly limited to, bathrooms, garages, outbuildings, outdoors, crawl spaces, unfinished basements, kitchens, garage-door openers, sump pumps, and stationery appliances. A good rule to follow is that if you are working in a damp or wet environment, then the receptacle you use should be GFCI-protected. If no GFCI receptacle is located nearby, then use an extension cord that has a built-in GFCI.

A GFCI receptacle resembles a conventional receptacle, except that it has built-in reset and test buttons. A GFCI can also be directly installed at the panel box as a circuit breaker. This type of ground-fault circuit interrupter has a test button only; when tripped, the switch flips only halfway off to break the circuit. To reset the circuit, the breaker must be switched completely off and then flipped back on again. A GFCI receptacle is less expensive than a breaker-type GFCI and has the advantage of letting you reset a circuit at the point of use.

A GFCI receptacle has both test and reset buttons. When a ground fault occurs or a test is made, the reset button will pop out. Once a fault is eliminated or the test completed, press the button back in to reset the circuit.

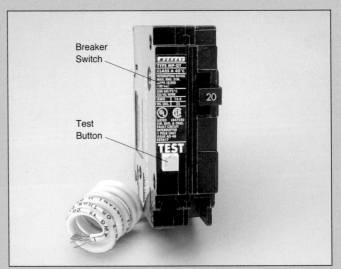

A GFCI circuit breaker has a test button, but no reset button. To reset a GFCI breaker, first push the switch to the off position; then flip it back to the on position.

Installing a GFCI Receptacle

Installing a GFCI receptacle isn't much harder than installing a standard receptacle. The only difference is that the GFCI has two sets of terminal screws, each with a different purpose. One is marked line and is used for the incoming power line. The other set is marked load and is used for the outgoing wires that connect to downstream receptacles in the circuit.

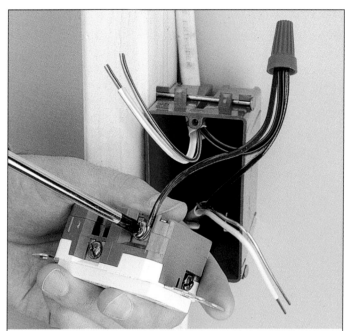

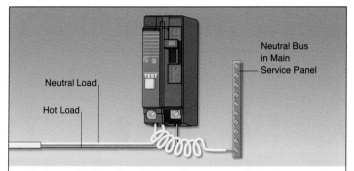

Neutral Bus in Main Service Panel

Neutral Load

Hot Load

TEST

20

To install the circuit breaker type of GFCI, simply insert the device into the panel box in the same way as a conventional circuit breaker; then connect the black and white load wires from the circuit you wish to protect. Connect the white corkscrew wire attached to the GFCI circuit breaker to the white neutral bus in the panel.

1 Pull both cables into the box, and strip the sheathing from the cable and the insulation from the ends of all the wires. Join the black cable wires with a black pigtail with a wire connector. Then attach the black pigtail to the HOT LINE terminal screw on the side of the GFCI receptacle.

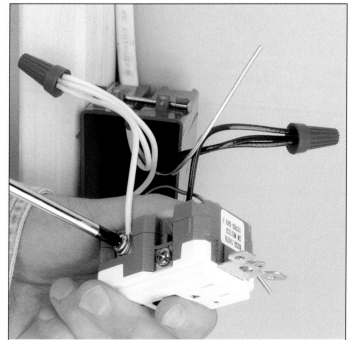

2 Join the white neutral wires from both cables with a white pigtail using a wire connector. Then securely attach the pigtail to the white line screw on the side of the receptacle.

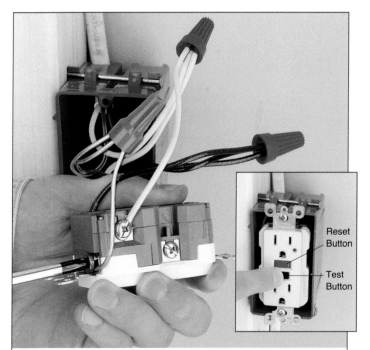

Reset Button

Test Button

3 Finish up the wire connections by joining the ground wires from the cables and a grounding pigtail with a wire connector. Then attach the pigtail to the receptacle's grounding screw. Install the receptacle, and test the reset button by pushing in the TEST button. The RESET button should pop out.

Switches

Single-Pole Switches

A switch controls the flow of power in a circuit. Single-pole switches have two screw terminals; it can control a circuit from one location only. Power is connected to one side of the switch at all times. When the switch is on, electricity flows from the wire attached to the powered screw terminal, through the switch, and into the fixture or appliance wiring connected to the other terminal.

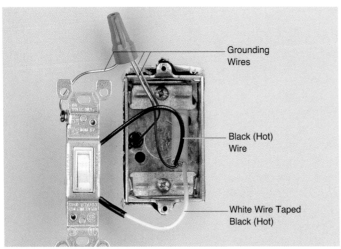

Grounding Wires

Black (Hot) Wire

White Wire Taped Black (Hot)

At the end of a circuit, both the black and white wires connecting to a switch are hot. To indicate this, wrap the white wire using black tape.

Single-Pole Switch Anatomy

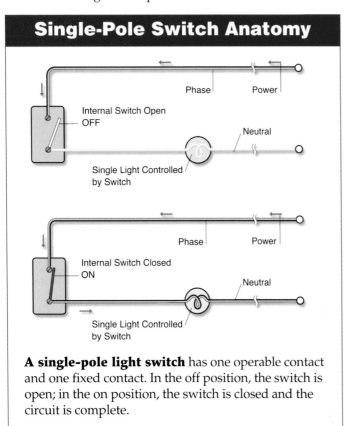

Phase   Power

Internal Switch Open
OFF

Neutral

Single Light Controlled by Switch

Phase   Power

Internal Switch Closed
ON

Neutral

Single Light Controlled by Switch

A single-pole light switch has one operable contact and one fixed contact. In the off position, the switch is open; in the on position, the switch is closed and the circuit is complete.

Single-Pole Switch to Light Fixture

In a standard lighting circuit, the power is supplied by a two-wire cable with a grounding wire. In this configuration, the light fixture is located at the end of the cable run.

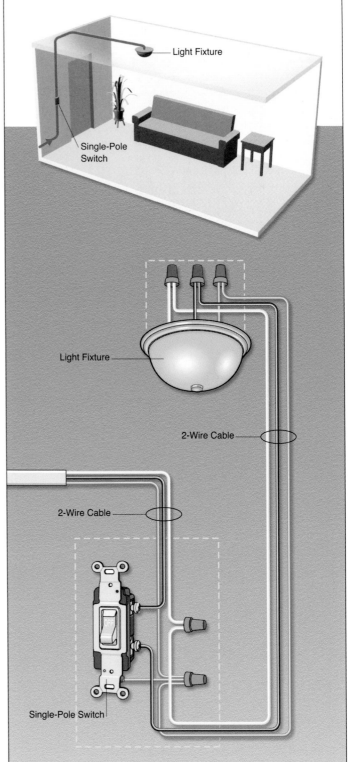

Light Fixture

Single-Pole Switch

Light Fixture

2-Wire Cable

2-Wire Cable

Single-Pole Switch

Wiring a Middle-of-Run Single-Pole Switch

Wiring a middle-of-run, single-pole switch is one of the easiest wiring projects. Only two cables come into the box. The white wires are joined with one wire connector, the ground wires are joined with a pigtail under another connector. The other end of the pigtail is attached to the ground screw on the switch. And the black wires (one from each cable) are attached to the two screw terminals on the switch. Remember, wires can come loose from terminal screws and wire connectors. To prevent bad connections at the terminals, make sure the wire hooks are flat against the fixture and that the screws are all tight. To make the best wire splices, strip off the insulation, then twist the ends together with pliers before you install the wire connector.

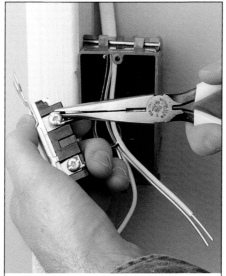

1 In a middle-of-run switch circuit the box contains two cables. Strip the sheathing from the cables and the insulation from the ends of the wires. Using long-nose pliers, form a hook at the end of both black wires, and attach these hooks to the screw terminals on the side of the switch.

2 Join the two white wires with a wire connector. Then join the two ground wires and a separate grounding pigtail together in another wire connector. If it's a metal box, join two pigtails to the grounding wires. One is attached to the metal box and the other to the grounding screw on the switch.

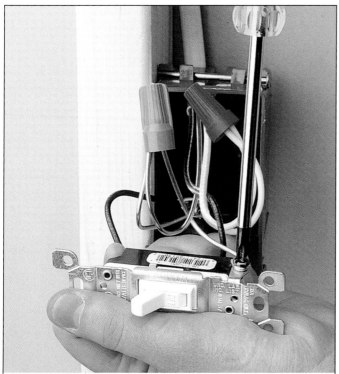

3 Form a hook on the end of the grounding pigtail, and attach it to the switch's grounding screw. Then carefully push the switch and the wiring back into the box, and attach the switch to the box using screws.

4 Test the circuit to make sure it works properly.

Light Fixture to an End-of-Run Single-Pole Switch

Use two-wire cable to wire a light fixture where the switch comes at the end of the cable run. This configuration is known as a switch loop. Mark the white neutral wire with black tape to indicate that it is hot.

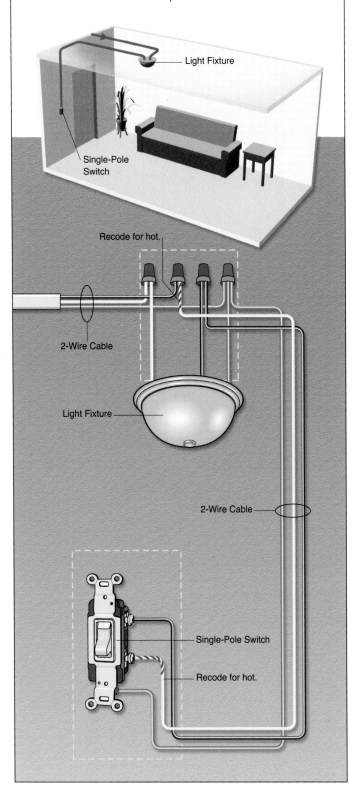

Recode for hot.

2-Wire Cable

Light Fixture

2-Wire Cable

Single-Pole Switch

Recode for hot.

Double-Ganged Switches to End-of-Run Light Fixtures

In this setup, power is fed first through the switches and then to the light fixtures. Only two-wire cable is needed for the wiring connections. The switches occupy one double-ganged electrical box.

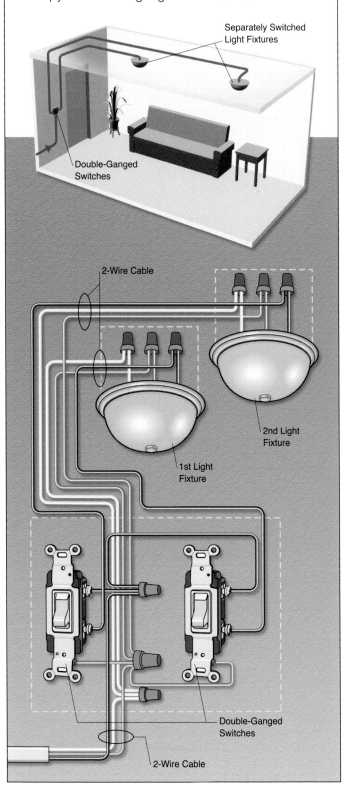

Separately Switched Light Fixtures

Double-Ganged Switches

2-Wire Cable

2nd Light Fixture

1st Light Fixture

Double-Ganged Switches

2-Wire Cable

Three-Way Switches

Like a single-pole switch, a three-way switch controls the flow of power in an electrical circuit, but from two different locations instead of just one. This type of switch is useful, for example, when you want to be able to turn on a stairway light from either the top or bottom of the stairway, or a detached garage light from either the house or the garage. Such switching requires special three-conductor or three-way switch cable with ground. This type of cable is usually round, rather than flat like conventional nonmetallic (NM) cable, and it contains an additional, insulated conductor—a red wire.

Three-way switches also differ from single-pole switches in that they have three screw terminals instead of two: a com terminal (dark screw), and two traveler screws to connect wires that run between switches. The switch also has a grounding screw. The switch does not have either an on or an off marked position because the com terminal alternates the connection between two different switch locations, allowing either position to potentially close the circuit.

You must consider three different cables when wiring a three-way switch: the feeder cable, the fixture cable, and the three-wire cable. The typical wiring method is to run the two-wire hot feeder cable into the first switch box, and then the three-way switch cable between the first and the second switch box. You can then run a second two-wire fixture cable between the second switch box and the fixture box. An alternative method is to run the hot feeder into one switch box; then run the three-way switch cable from the first switch box to the light fixture and then to the second switch box. Either method initially requires that you run the hot feeder to a switch box. It's also possible to run power first to the light fixture, but this method is not preferred because it's more difficult to troubleshoot if there's a problem in the circuit.

Three-Way Switch Anatomy

SWITCHES A AND B BOTH OPEN

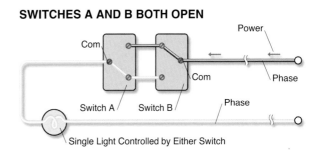

Single Light Controlled by Either Switch

SWITCH A CLOSES CIRCUIT

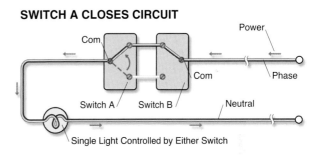

Single Light Controlled by Either Switch

SWITCH B CLOSES CIRCUIT

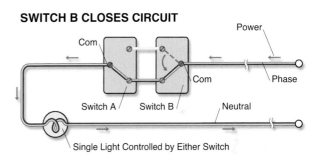

Single Light Controlled by Either Switch

A three-way light switch has one operable contact and two fixed contacts. In the first position, the switch is open; in the second position, the switch is closed and the circuit is completed through switch box A; in the third position, the switch is also closed but the circuit is completed through switch box B.

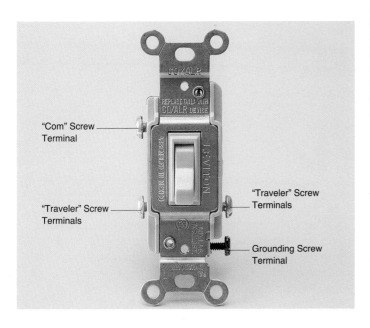

"Com" Screw Terminal

"Traveler" Screw Terminals

"Traveler" Screw Terminals

Grounding Screw Terminal

A three-way switch has three terminal screws and no on/off positions. The dark colored screw terminal screw is the com, or common, terminal. The two light screw terminals are switch leads, known as "travelers."

Wiring a Three-Way Switch

There are many different ways to install three-way switches but one of the most popular is shown here. The power is brought to one switch box with a 2-wire (with ground) cable. The box is connected to the second switch box with 3-wire (with ground) cable. The circuit is completed with 2-wire (with ground) cable going from the second switch box to the light fixture. The three-wire cable has a red wire in addition to the standard black, white, and ground wires. The hardest thing about wiring a three-way switch is to keep track of the common wires and the traveler wires. The common wire is the black wire from the cable that supplies power to the circuit. It is screwed to the common terminal. The traveler wires are the black and red wires from the three-wire cable that joins the two switches. These wires are screwed to the traveler terminals.

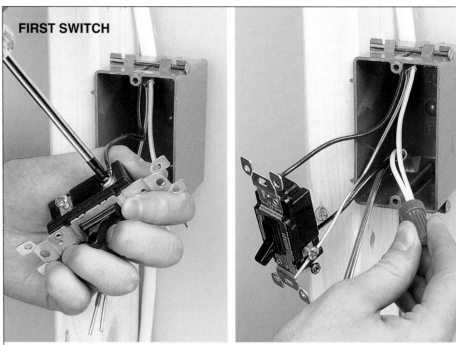

FIRST SWITCH

1 First, bring a two-wire power cable and a three-wire cable that goes between the switches into the box. Strip the sheathing and wire insulation from both cables and all wires. Then attach the black wire from the power cable to the common screw terminal (left). Join the white wires with a wire connector (right).

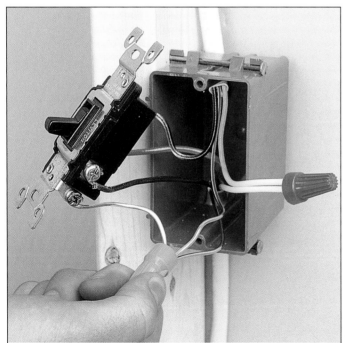

4 Join the ground wires from the two cables to a grounding pigtail wire using a wire connector. Attach the other end of the grounding pigtail to the green grounding screw on the switch. Push the switch and all the wires into the box, and attach the switch to the box using screws.

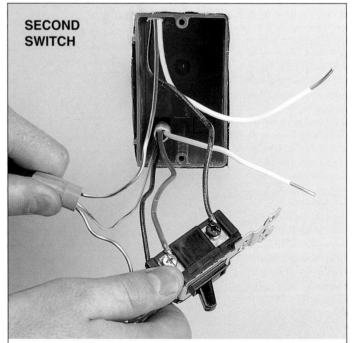

SECOND SWITCH

5 Strip the sheathing from the cables and the insulation from the wires, and attach the black common wire to the common terminal. Then attach the black and red wires, from the three-wire cable, to the traveler terminals. Join the ground wires to the grounding screw using a pigtail and a wire connector.

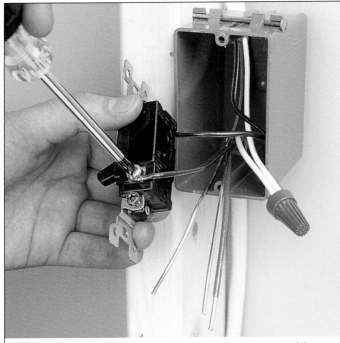

2 Connect the black wire from the three-wire cable to one of the traveler terminals on the first switch. When you install the second three-way switch, attach the other end of this black wire to the same traveler terminal on the second switch.

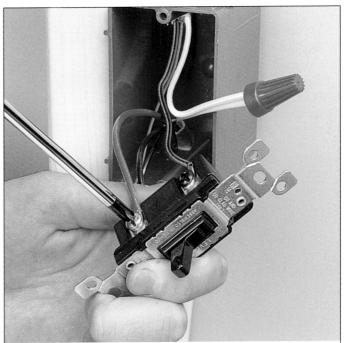

3 Attach the red wire from the three-wire cable to the remaining traveler terminal. As with the black traveler, the other end of this red wire should be attached to the same traveler terminal on the second three-way switch.

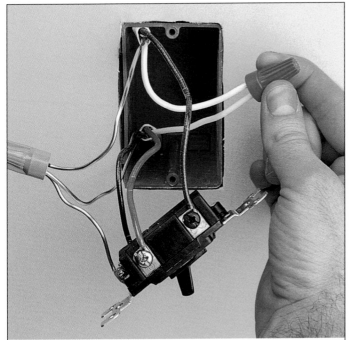

6 Join the white neutral wires from both cables using a wire connector. Push the switch and all the wires into the box, and attach the switch to the box using screws.

7 Complete the circuit by attaching the cable wires to fixture wires using wire connectors, white-to-white, black-to-black, and ground-to-ground. Attach the light fixture to the ceiling box. Then turn on the circuit power, and test the switches.

Three-Way Switches with Fixture at End-of-Run

In this switch circuit, power goes from the first switch box through the second, and then to the light fixture. A three-wire cable with ground is run between the switches and a two-wire cable runs between the second switch and the fixture.

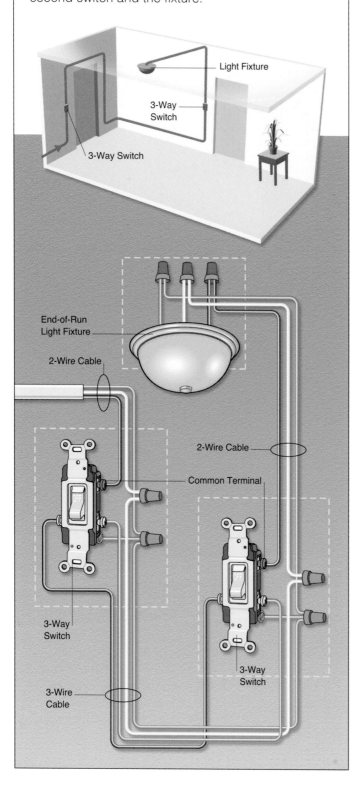

Light Fixture

3-Way Switch

3-Way Switch

End-of-Run Light Fixture

2-Wire Cable

2-Wire Cable

Common Terminal

3-Way Switch

3-Way Switch

3-Wire Cable

Three-Way Switches with Fixture at Start-of-Run

In this setup, power enters the light fixture on a two-wire grounded cable. It proceeds to the three-way switches and then returns to the fixture. Two-wire cable connects the fixture to the first switch and three-wire cable runs between the switches.

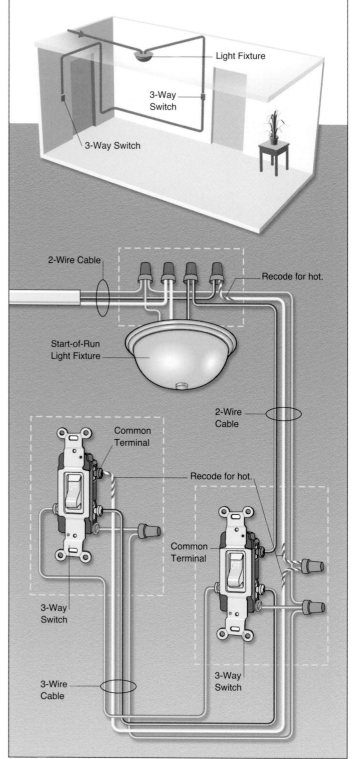

Light Fixture

3-Way Switch

3-Way Switch

2-Wire Cable

Recode for hot.

Start-of-Run Light Fixture

2-Wire Cable

Common Terminal

Recode for hot.

Common Terminal

3-Way Switch

3-Way Switch

3-Wire Cable

Three-Way Switches with Fixture at Middle-of-Run

Here, the light fixture is positioned between the two three-way switches. Power comes to the first switch on a two-wire grounded cable. It passes through the light fixture, proceeds to the second switch, and then returns to the fixture on three-wire cable.

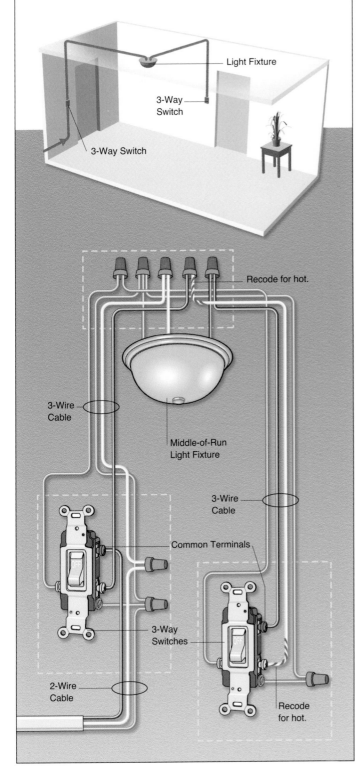

Recode for hot.

3-Wire Cable

3-Wire Cable

Common Terminals

Middle-of-Run Light Fixture

3-Way Switches

2-Wire Cable

Recode for hot.

Start-of-Run Fixture between Three-Way Switches

In this hookup, power comes to the light fixture box and is then connected to the three way switches, which are powered on separate lines from opposite sides of the fixture. The white feeder wire connects directly to the silver screw terminal of the fixture.

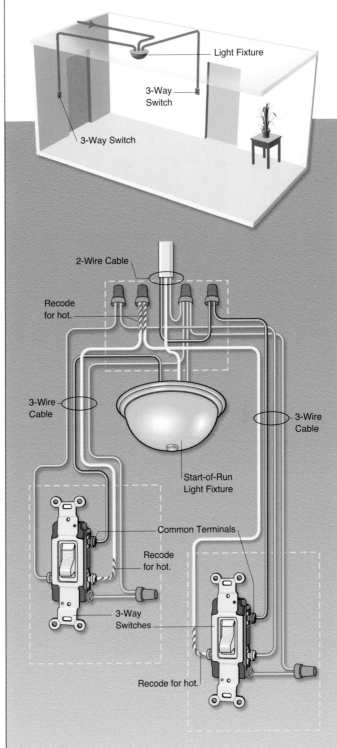

2-Wire Cable

Recode for hot.

3-Wire Cable

3-Wire Cable

Start-of-Run Light Fixture

Common Terminals

Recode for hot.

3-Way Switches

Recode for hot.

chapter 5
lighting

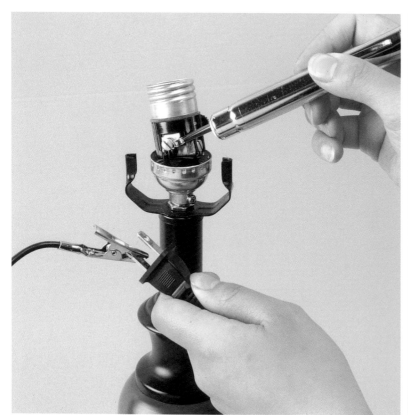

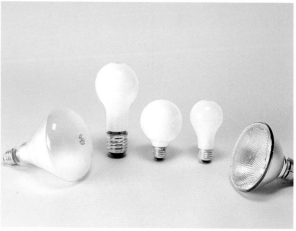

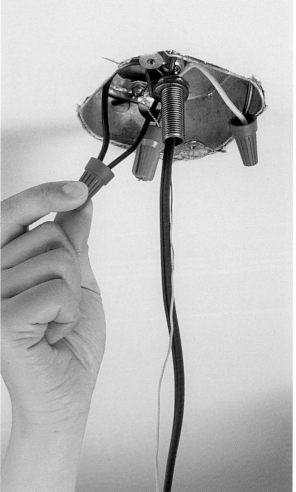

Plugs, Cords, and Sockets

Standard Plugs

Plugs come in a variety of different styles and shapes, including flat- or round-corded, grounded, polarized, and quick-connect. Round-corded plugs are typically used on larger appliances that require three-pronged, grounded plugs; smaller appliances commonly use flat-corded plugs. A polarized plug has one wide and one narrow prong and can only be inserted into a receptacle so that the neutral and hot cord wires properly align with the neutral and hot receptacle wires.

Some homeowners may still be using fixtures that have older-style, permanently attached cords and plugs. Because such cords and plugs no longer meet NEC standards, it is simply cheaper and safer for you to replace them, rather than attempting to repair them. When you do replace a plug or cord, be sure that the new device

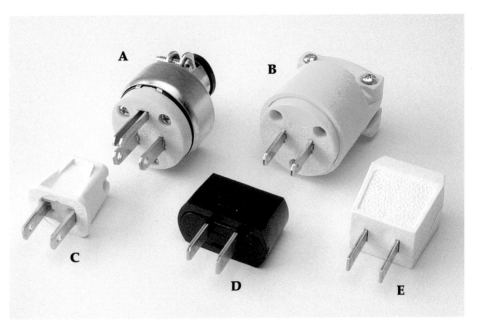

Plugs come in various configurations for different purposes; be sure that the replacement plugs you buy are appropriate for the appliances, receptacles, or wires to which they will be connected. **A**–grounded round-cord plug; **B**–round-cord plug; **C**–quick-connect plug; **D**–polarized plug; **E**–flat-cord plug

meets current code requirements (NEC Article 406). If your existing cord is in good condition, but the plug needs to be replaced, cut the cord just behind the plug, and strip the insulation off the end of the cut wires. Then properly reconnect them to the new plug.

How Much Light Do You Need?

Type	Incandescent	Fluorescent	Location
General (ambient) Lighting	2–4 watts per square foot of area. Double this if counters, cabinets, or flooring are dark	1–1½ watts per square foot of floor area	90 inches above the floor
Task Lighting			
Cleanup Centers	150 watts	30–40 watts	25 inches above the sink
Countertops	75–100 watts for each 3 running feet of work surface	20 watts for each 3 running feet of work surface	14–22 inches above the work surface
Cooking Centers	150 watts	30–40 watts	18–25 inches above burners Most range hoods have lights.
Dining Tables	100–120 watts	Not applicable	25–30 inches above the table

Replacing a Standard Round-Cord Plug

Most extension cords these days have integral, molded plugs on both ends. So if one of these plugs is damaged, you have to cut it off and replace it with a separate plug. These are common hardware store and home center items. To make sure you get the right plug, cut off a 6-inch length of the cord and take it with you to the store. This will allow you to compare the size and type of your cord with the plugs that are available. You can use lineman's pliers or diagonal cutting pliers, like we used, to cut off the ends of the cord. Then strip the cord sheathing so about 2 inches of the wires are exposed. You can use dedicated strippers for this job, or just make the cut carefully using a utility knife. The amount of sheathing you remove is based on the design of the plug you buy. Its package should tell how much sheathing to remove.

1 Damaged extension cord plugs, such as this one with the missing ground prong, should be replaced. If the cord has a separate plug, just remove the old plug. If the cord has an integral cord, cut off the plug.

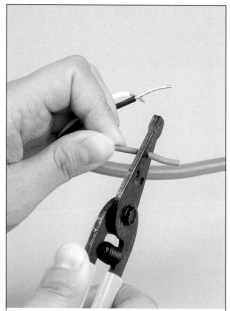

2 Strip the cable sheathing and the wire insulation using a multipurpose tool.

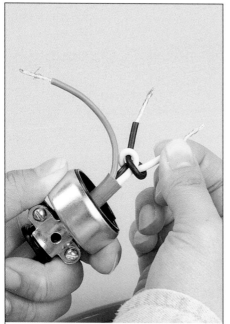

3 Slide the plug over the end of the wire, and tie the white and black wires together as shown. This knot, called an Underwriter's Knot, is designed to reduce the chance that pulling on the cord will pull the wires off their plug terminals.

4 Attach the white wire to the silver screw, the black wire to the brass screw, and the ground wire to the grounding screw.

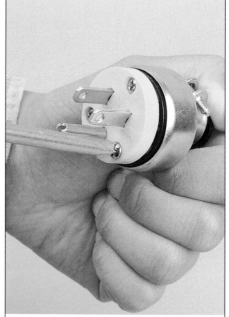

5 Pull the prongs back into the plug body; then attach the plug cover over the prongs. Finish up by tightening the cable clamp screws so the plug is securely attached to the cable.

Installing a Quick-Disconnect Plug

The most common extension cord for home use is the flat cable type that matches the cable found on just about every floor and table lamp that's sold these days. Because there are so many of these cords in use, fixing them has become easy because manufacturers have created so many clever solutions. Probably the best is the simple quick-connect plug. All that's required is to cut off the old plug and slide the cut wire into the new plug and you're done.

1 Flat cords with integral plugs like this can't be repaired when the plug fails. The only option is to cut off the plug and install a new separate plug. If you chose a quick-connect plug, you don't even need to strip the insulation from the wire.

PRO TIP

There are several reasons that a light fixture can flicker. To check the cord, turn on the light and flex the cord. If the light flickers, the cord is faulty and needs to be replaced. (See page 82.)

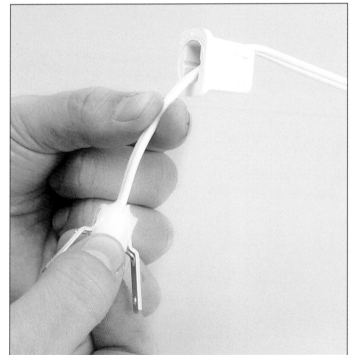

2 The quick-connect plug comes in two pieces: the plug housing and the prong assembly that goes into the housing. The housing goes on the cable first. Then insert the cable into the prong assembly following the directions on the product packaging.

3 Squeeze the prongs together with the cable inside. Barbs on the sides of the prongs will pierce the wire insulation and make contact with the wires. Then pull the housing over the prong assembly until the two snap together.

Replacing a Lamp Cord

Whenever you replace a plug, you should also check the cord. If it's worn or damaged, then replace it, too. Although a cord with an integral plug is preferable, you can purchase cord by the foot and attach a plug to it so that you get the length of cord you want. In either case, select a cord that is appropriate for the appliance and that matches the original type of cord—do not use a light-duty cord in place of a heavy duty one. Also, if the appliance is metal, the cord should contain a green grounding wire. To gain access to the wiring inside the lamp, remove the bottom of the lamp. In some cases, the base is screwed to the lamp. But in others the base is made of stiff cardboard covered with felt to protect the surface where the lamp is used. This panel can be removed by sliding a utility knife around the perimeter and prying it off. When the job is done, reattach it with white glue.

1 Whenever you replace a damaged plug, take the time to examine the whole cord for other damage. If you find any cracked, frayed, or dried sections where the wires are exposed, replace the entire cord.

2 To remove the cord, untie the knot at the top, and pull it out through the bottom of the lamp.

3 Feed the new cable into the bottom of the lamp and up through the socket base. Strip about ½ in. of insulation from the end of both wires.

4 Pull the two wires apart so there's enough free wire to tie an Underwriters' knot. Once the knot is tied, push the wire down into the socket so just the ends stick up.

5 Attach the copper wire to the brass terminal screw and the silver wire to the silver terminal screw. Then reassemble the socket; install a bulb; and plug it into a receptacle.

Light Sockets and Switches

Occasionally, you may have a problem with a faulty light socket or switch. To test a socket, first unplug the lamp. Next, remove the socket from the lamp; then separate it from its outer shell and insulating sleeve. Clip a continuity tester to the socket shell; then touch the probe to the neutral (silver) terminal screw. If the tester lights, the continuity of the circuit is unbroken. To test the switch, clip the tester to the brass terminal screw; then touch the probe to the brass tab inside the socket shell. If the tester does not light in either switch position, the switch needs to be replaced.

If a lamp has no metal parts that must be grounded, then a zip cord with only two wires may be used to wire its socket and switch. This type of cord has one ribbed side and one smooth side; the ribbed side contains the

Socket and Switch Anatomy

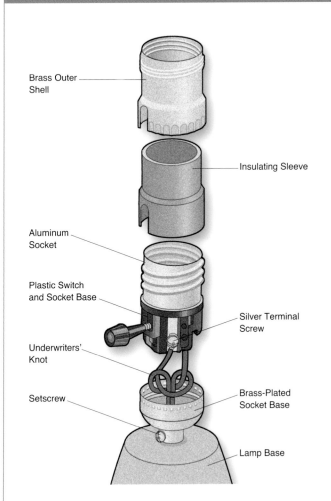

- Brass Outer Shell
- Insulating Sleeve
- Aluminum Socket
- Plastic Switch and Socket Base
- Silver Terminal Screw
- Underwriters' Knot
- Setscrew
- Brass-Plated Socket Base
- Lamp Base

A lamp socket that has a built-in switch is illustrated above. If either the socket or the switch is faulty, it is best to replace them both; if the cord is damaged, then replace it too.

Testing Sockets and Switches

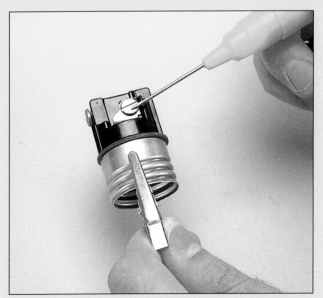

To test a socket, clip a continuity tester to the socket; then touch the probe to the silver (neutral) terminal screw.

To test the switch, clamp the tester to the brass (hot) terminal screw, and touch the probe to the brass tab in the socket. The tester will light if connections are not broken.

neutral wire and connects to the silver terminal screw. The smooth side contains the hot wire and connects to the brass screw terminal. This difference aids in maintaining the correct polarity of all the wiring and fixture components—neutral to neutral, hot to hot. A reversal of polarity can result in a shock hazard, even when the lamp is switched off.

Replacing a Fluorescent Ballast

Fluorescent lighting is generally a better deal than incandescent lighting because it delivers more light per watt of electricity. Unfortunately, this efficiency doesn't tell the whole story. Fluorescent fixtures have ballasts that incandescent fixtures don't have, and when these wear out, they need to be replaced, usually at about $20 each.

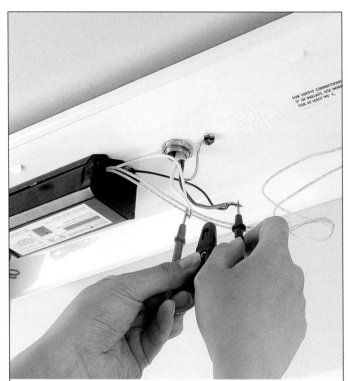

1 First, disconnect the power to the light circuit that serves the fixture. Then remove the light diffuser, the bulbs, and the metal cover plate.

2 Remove the wire connectors from the power leads, and use a circuit tester to verify that the circuit power is off.

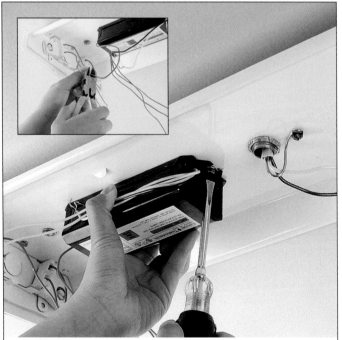

3 Cut the wires that extend from the ballast to the bulb sockets on both ends of the fixture (inset). Then remove the screw that holds the ballast in place. Be sure to hold the ballast with your other hand when the screw is removed. This device is heavy and can do some damage if it's allowed to drop.

4 Install the new ballast, and make sure the mounting screw is tight. Then strip the insulation off the cut wires, and join these to the ballast wires with wire connectors. To prevent these wires from being pinched when the metal cover is installed, tape the wires to the fixture.

Replacing a Fluorescent Fixture

Because fluorescent fixtures are very durable, they don't usually need to be replaced because they don't work anymore. When they are replaced, it's often because people want something that looks more residential and less industrial, which was the case here. The hardest part of this job is repairing the old-fixture mounting holes in the ceiling and touching up the paint so it's not noticeable afterwards.

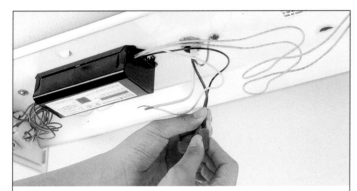

1 Turn off the power to the circuit that serves the fluorescent fixture. Then remove the light diffuser, the lamps, and the fixture cover. Remove the wire connectors from the power wires, and verify that power is off using a neon circuit tester.

2 Remove the cable connector that holds the power cable to the fixture by unthreading the locknut in a counterclockwise direction.

3 Remove the screw, or other fasteners, that hold the fixture to the ceiling, and set the old fixture aside.

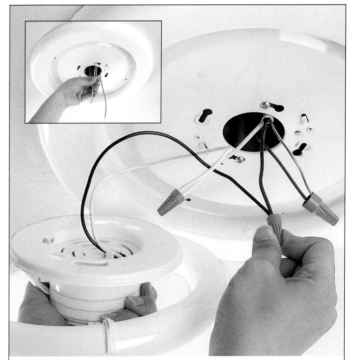

4 Install the new fixture base over the ceiling box. In this case, it just hangs from the box screws (inset). Then hold the new light next to the base, and connect the power wires to the fixture wires with wire connectors. Push the wires into the box, and install the fixture.

Installing a Fluorescent Dimmer Switch

Everybody knows how convenient a dimmer switch is for standard incandescent bulbs. With a turn of a knob you can change the amount of light in any room from bright to practically dark. The same capability is available for fluorescent lights, but it costs a lot more and takes more time to install than the simple dimmer switch that we've all used. You can get a cheap incandescent dimmer for about $15. A fluorescent unit, on the other hand, will probably cost over $50, and you'll have to replace the ballast in your light unit, which adds to the cost. Still in some situations, having the dimming capability for fluorescent units is more than worth the trouble. Installation isn't too hard, but it does require that you install a three-wire-plus-ground cable from the wall switch to the light fixture.

PRO TIP

Recycling a Ballast

There is nothing more responsible for the mess in the basement or the garage than the impulse to keep something for a rainy day, only to find out 10 years later that the weather never got that bad. A fluorescent ballast, however, is not something that should be thrown out. If you replace a standard ballast with a dimmable unit, hold onto the old one for future use.

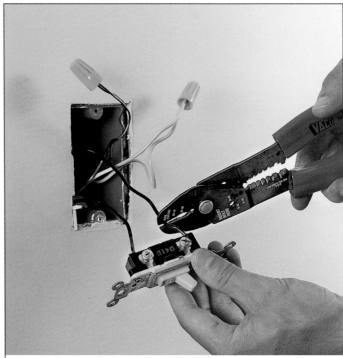

1 Turn off the power to the fixture at the service panel; then take off the switch cover and pull out the switch. Loosen the terminal screws to free the wires, or cut them off close to the switch using wire strippers.

4 Join all the whites wires, then all the ground wires. Next, join the black wires from the switch and the power line, the red switch lead to the black fixture wire, and the orange switch lead to the red fixture wire. Refer to directions that come with the switch.

5 Remove the existing ballast from the fixture housing. Ballasts are usually held in place with just a couple of screws. You can remove the ballast wires from the bulb sockets, or just cut the wires and use twist connectors to join the new ballast to the socket wires.

2 Feed a fish tape into the switch box, and tape the end of a three-wire-with-ground cable onto the end of the fish tape.

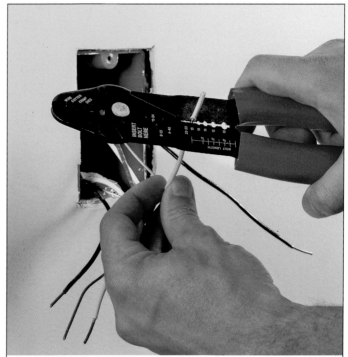

3 Once the new cable has been fished to the fluorescent fixture, prepare the wires in the switch box so the new dimmer switch can be installed. Strip the insulation off the ends of all the wires.

6 Install the new dimmable ballast by driving screws into the fixture housing. The old screw holes may work, but if they are located in the wrong spot for the new unit, just drill new pilot holes, and use them for the ballast mounting screws.

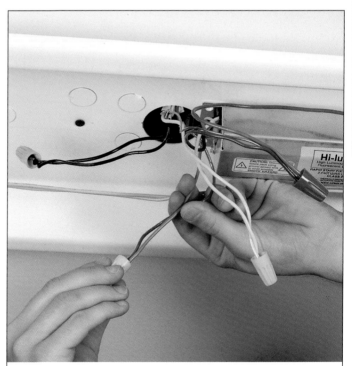

7 Join the ballast wires to the switch wires with twist connectors. The white wires go together, as do the blacks and ground wires. The orange ballast wire is joined to the red switch wire.

Surface-Mounted Fixtures

Surface-mounted fixtures are usually installed on a ceiling or wall. They may use incandescent, fluorescent, or quartz halogen bulbs. Wall sconces, globe lights, above-vanity strip lighting, and ceiling fixtures are all examples of this type of lighting. Surface-mounted lights are generally attached to lighting outlet boxes.

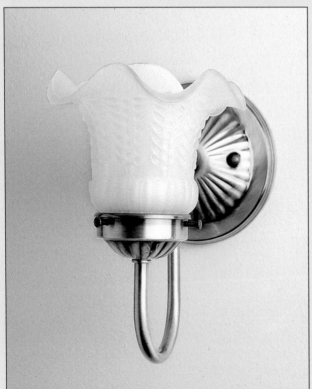

Surface-mounted fixtures come in a variety of styles appropriate for ceiling or wall installation.

Installing a Ceiling-Mounted Fixture

The hardest part of this job is getting the box installed and pulling the cable to the box location. Once both are in place, strip the sheathing and wire insulation from the cable, and screw a light fixture-hanging strap to the box. Join the wires from the fixture and the cable using wire connectors. Then tighten the fixture in place; install the proper light bulb (or bulbs); and screw on the fixture globe.

PRO TIP

A typical incandescent lightbulb has a life span of about 900 to 1000 hours. At roughly 5 hours per day, that's means about 6 months of life. Compact fluorescent bulbs, on the other hand, can last up to 8000 hours while using about 25 percent of the energy that incandescent use (for the same amount of light output). CF bulbs are more expensive, typically 4–5 times as much as incandescents. But in the long run they are much cheaper, which makes them worth considering as a replacement whenever an incandescent bulb burns out.

3 Screw a threaded pipe nipple into the collar of the hanging strip. After the fixture is installed, you'll thread another nut onto the bottom of this nipple that will hold the fixture securely in place. Make sure the threads are clean so the fixture nut is easy to install.

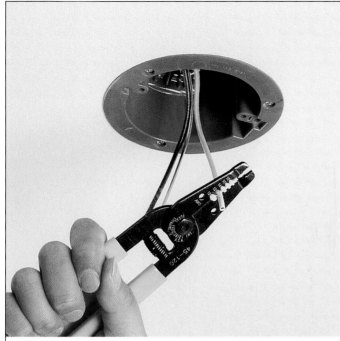

1 Begin by cutting a box hole in the ceiling and fishing new cable from the switch box into the ceiling opening. Install a retrofit ceiling box, and tighten the support wings against the drywall. Remove the cable sheathing, and strip the ends of the wires using wire strippers.

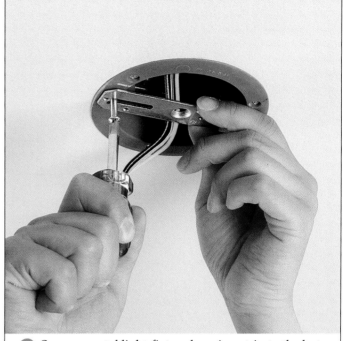

2 Screw a metal light-fixture hanging strip to the bottom of the box. This strap provides threaded holes for mounting different fixtures.

4 Join the fixture wires to the cable wires by combining like-colored wires and securing using wire connectors. Add a short pigtail wire to the ground wires, and then tighten this pigtail wire under a green grounding screw. If possible, have someone hold the fixture while you make these connections.

5 Slide the fixture over the box, and turn the retaining nut onto the threaded nipple. Tighten the nut until the fixture is against the ceiling. Add the recommended bulbs, and install the globe that came with the fixture. Do not use bulbs with more wattage than the manufacturer recommends.

Installing Track Lighting

Track Lighting

If you want to try some track lighting to change the look of your kitchen or to direct more task lighting where you need it, then you're in luck. Installing one of these systems is not difficult, especially if you already have a switch-operated ceiling fixture. Just remove the old fixture; install the track; and slide the light heads into place.

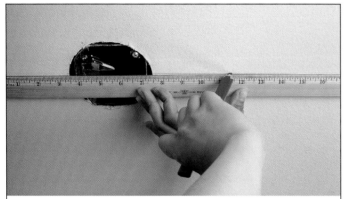

1 Turn off the power at the service panel, and remove the old ceiling fixture. Mark the ceiling for the location of the tracks.

2 Thread the wires from the power connector through the mounting-plate holes. Then connect like-colored wires from the connector to those in the ceiling box.

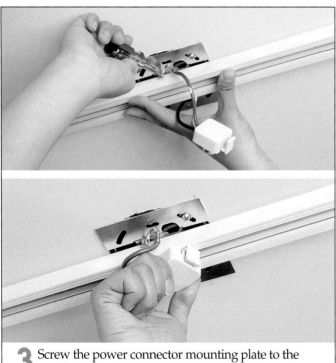

3 Screw the power connector mounting plate to the electrical box. Make sure the plate is tight and doesn't pinch any of the cable or fixture wires. Then lift up a section of track; slide it between the connector wires; and attach it temporarily to the mounting plate (top). Push the connector into the track, and twist-lock it in place.

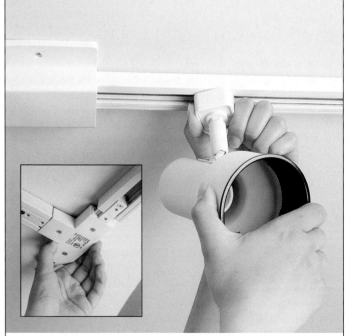

4 Install the tracks and any T- or L-connectors, and make sure they are all tight against the ceiling (inset). Slide the light fixtures onto the track, and lock them in place. Turn on the lights, and adjust the direction of the lamps if necessary.

Installing a Chandelier

Chandeliers

Hanging a chandelier differs from installing a ceiling-mounted light fixture because of the added weight of the fixture. This requires modifying the ceiling box to accommodate the extra weight. Special chandelier-hanging hardware is used for this purpose, including a threaded stud and nipple, a hickey, and locknuts. If you're replacing an existing light fixture, you'll have to beef up the box-hanging hardware.

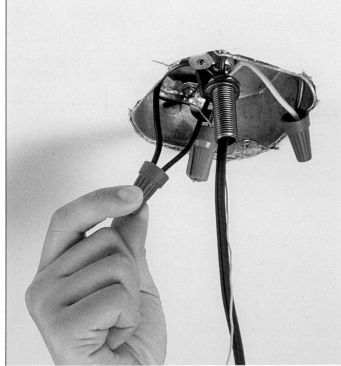

1 Turn off the circuit power to the existing light fixture at the service panel. Then remove the screws that hold the fixture in place, and unthread the wire connectors that join the circuit and fixtures wires.

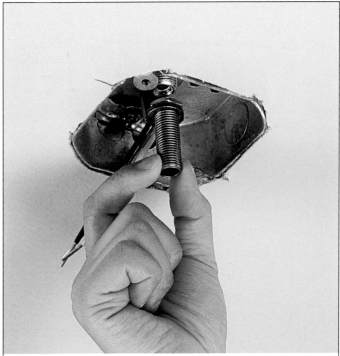

2 Make sure the electrical box is securely mounted to the ceiling framing. Then remove the center knockout plate; install a stud in the knockout hole; screw a hickey into the stud and a nipple into the hickey.

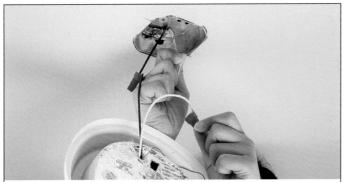

3 Have someone hold the chandelier or support it on a stepladder while you work. Thread the chandelier wires through the threaded nipple. Then connect the fixture wires to the box wires.

4 Once the wires are joined, slide the chandelier escutcheon plate up against the ceiling box. Hold it in place as you screw the collar nut onto the threaded nipple in the middle of the box.

chapter 6
specialty wiring

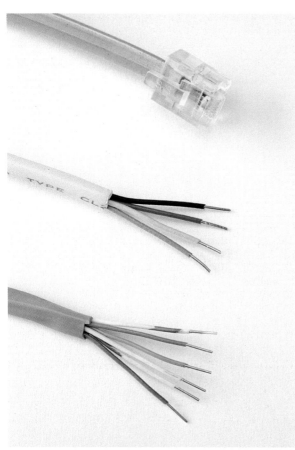

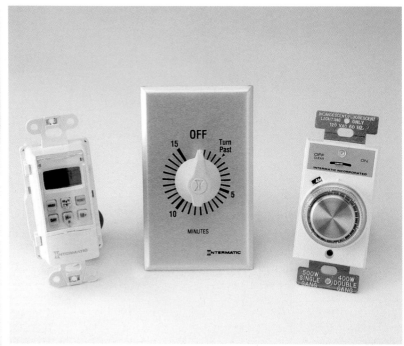

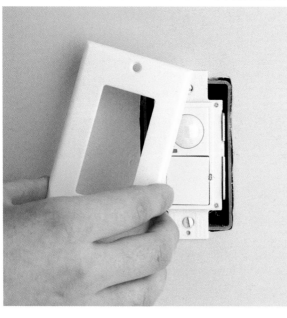

SO FAR STANDARD 120- AND 240-VOLT residential circuits have been discussed. Many devices used in contemporary homes, however, require much less voltage to operate. Such devices include but are not limited to bells, chimes, timers, sensors, alarms, thermostats, antennas, and telecommunications equipment. Because low-voltage wiring presents few hazards, it is barely touched upon by the NEC, except as it pertains to recreational vehicles and RV parks.

Low-Voltage Power

What It Is and How It Works

Low-voltage power is defined as 30 volts or less supplied through a transformer, a device that reduces standard 120-volt house current to the current required to power low-voltage equipment. A transformer may be mounted near or be directly attached to a junction box. In either case, the low-voltage wiring is connected to the transformer, which is in turn connected to the 120-volt wiring in the junction box. The current is converted as it passes from the box through the transformer and proceeds from the transformer to the low-voltage switch and/or device.

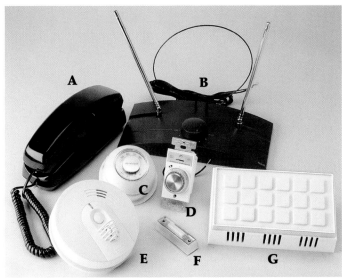

Specialty devices, such as timer controls and heat detectors, use standard 120-volt current. Low-voltage devices, such as chimes, telephones, and thermostats, use 30 volts or less. **A**–telephone; **B**–TV antenna; **C**–thermostat; **D**–timer control; **E**–smoke detector; **F**–doorbell; **G**–door chimes

Power is provided to low-voltage equipment by means of a step-down transformer that reduces standard 120-volt current to the lower voltage required. **A**–24-volt transformer; **B**–16-volt transformer; **C**–8- to 24-volt transformer

Time-Control Switches

Because a time-delay switch, unlike a clock-timer switch, does not require a neutral connection, it can be installed either in the middle or at the end of a wire run. Instead of three wires coming off the switch, there will only be two. Connect the black lead wires from the timer to the black hot wires from the circuit and fixture cables; then splice the two neutral circuit wires. Pigtail the bare copper grounding wires from the cables to the grounding screw in the switch box, if the box is metal. A digital-control switch is typically installed in the same way.

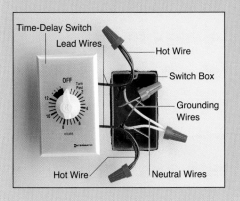

Time-Delay Switch
Lead Wires
Hot Wire
Switch Box
Grounding Wires
OFF Turn Past
Hot Wire
Neutral Wires

A time-delay switch operates a device for a given period of time, as opposed to operating it at a specified time.

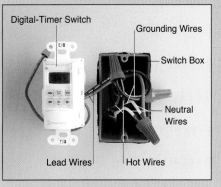

Digital-Timer Switch
Grounding Wires
Switch Box
Neutral Wires
Lead Wires
Hot Wires

A digital timer switch is programmable, allowing you to set multiple on/off cycles during the day. Cycles may be set at either regular or random intervals.

Installing a Low-Voltage Transformer

Low-Voltage Transformers

Transformers are usually composed of two tightly wound coils of wire. Because the coils, known as primary and secondary windings, are close together, as a current passes through the primary winding, magnetic flow produces another current in the secondary winding. In a low-voltage or step-down transformer, the primary coil—rated at 120 volts—has more windings than the secondary coil. A reduction in windings results in a proportional reduction in voltage, with the secondary coil usually providing 8 to 24 volts.

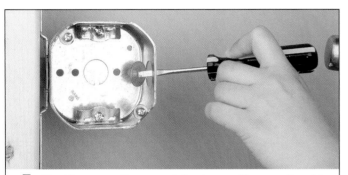

1 Start by mounting a metal octagonal box on the side of a stud or joist. Then remove the knockout plate on the side of the box.

2 Bring the circuit wire into the box, and tighten the box clamp or install a cable clamp. Strip the sheathing from the cable and the insulation from the wires.

3 Slide the transformer wires through the knockout hole, and mount the transformer on the box using the nut that's provided. If the insulation hasn't been stripped from the ends of the transformer wires, do it now.

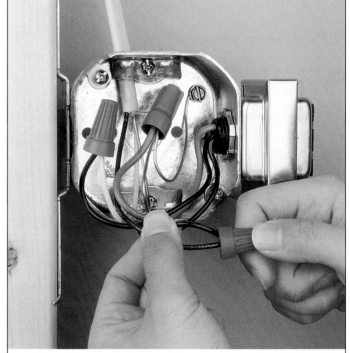

4 Join the two black transformer wires to the white and black circuit wires with using connectors. Join the ground wires from the circuit and the transformer to a grounding pigtail using a wire connector. Attach the other end of the pigtail to the grounding screw inside the box.

Low-Voltage Wire and Cable

Wire Type		Description	Gauge	Typical Usage
	Lamp Cord *Zip Cord*	Two insulated wires that can be pulled or "zipped" apart	18	Lamps, small appliances, cords
	Flat Ribbon Cable	Several insulated, color-coded wires that can be "zipped" apart	24	Computer circuit/ serial bus connections for keyboards, scanners, printers
	Bell Wire	Single or multistranded, insulated, color coded	18	Bells, chimes, thermostats, timers, control circuits
	Video Coaxial Cable	A single insulated wire wrapped by a foil and braided shield	RG-59 *22-Gauge Core*	Television antenna connections, home entertainment
		Quad-shielded cable containing 2 foil shields, 2 braided shields	RG-6 *18-Gauge Core*	Cable, satellite television antenna connections, home entertainment
	D-Station Cable	Cable containing four insulated, color-coded wires	24–28	Permanent, indoor, home-telephone wiring
	Category 5 Cable	Cable containing four pairs of insulated, color-coded wires	24	Increased circuit capacity for home computer, telecommunications

Low-voltage wires and cables are available in a variety of types and gauges that are suitable for different purposes, including wiring bells and chimes, telecommunications equipment, and home theater.

Low-Voltage Wire

Because it carries such low secondary power, low-voltage wiring requires only a thin layer of plastic insulation. Low-voltage wiring may consist of a single conductor or multiple conductors wrapped in cable. This type of wiring encompasses a variety of uses from connecting simple bells and chimes to wiring sophisticated home theater, telecommunications, and computer networking systems. (See the table, above, "Low-Voltage Wire and Cable.") Typically, low-voltage wires extend in size from 14 gauge down to 24 gauge (AWG) and even smaller. The NEC does not permit this type of wiring to run in the same raceways, conduits, or cables as wires carrying normal voltage (Article 725). In addition, low-voltage wires may not occupy any electrical box containing higher voltage

wiring, unless the box is properly partitioned. Low-voltage wires must generally be separated from higher-voltage wiring by 2 inches or more.

Low-voltage wires can be fished, stapled, and spliced the same way as conventional wiring. In some ways, more care should be taken with low-voltage wires because most of them are small gauge and more fragile. Just as full-voltage wire must be joined at screw terminals or be spliced inside a junction box, low-voltage wires must be connected or spliced inside a terminal jack or other type of specialized coupling device. Today, most electronic equipment comes with its own specialized wiring and terminal connectors to make properly insulated splices. Common connectors are also available and are usually color-coded red for 22- to 18-gauge wire and blue for 16- to 14-gauge wire.

Wiring Applications

Bells and Chimes

Although modern homes are more likely to have chimes than doorbells or buzzers, their wiring systems are essentially the same. Because a doorbell or chime needs less than 120 volts of power to operate, you will have to install a step-down transformer to reduce house voltage to 24 volts. Some systems, however, may need as little as 15 volts. (See "Installing a Low-Voltage Transformer," on page 94.) Be sure to use a transformer that is right for the signal system you are installing.

Once a low-voltage transformer is in place, you must make three separate connections to complete the doorbell or chime circuit. The push button is the switch that, when pressed, completes the circuit by ringing the signal.

Doorbell Circuits

ONE PUSH BUTTON, ONE SIGNAL DEVICE

Signal Device (Bell or Chime)

Low-Voltage Transformer

Push-Button Switch

TWO PUSH BUTTONS, ONE SIGNAL DEVICE

Push-Button Switch

Low-Voltage Transformer

Signal Device (Bell or Chime)

Push-Button Switch

ONE PUSH BUTTON, MULTIPLE SIGNAL DEVICES

Multiple Signal Devices

Low-Voltage Transformer

Push-Button Switch

Installing Door Chimes

The busier your house is, the more you need door chimes. A simple door knocker may have worked when you were a kid, but it doesn't stand a chance against a home theater system or any number of kitchen appliances. Fortunately, installing chimes isn't very hard and requires only common tools.

PRO TIP

Testing Door Chimes

After installation, press each button. If the chimes sound, the installation is complete. If the push-button switches don't work, the problem is with either the transformer or the wiring between the transformer and the chimes. If one button works but the other doesn't, the trouble is in the switch or the wiring connecting the switch to the chimes unit. If the transformer makes no humming sound, it may be faulty or the circuit may be dead. To test the circuit, touch the probes on a multi-tester to the ends of the circuit wires when the circuit is on. If the multi-tester does not detect power within 2 volts of its rating, replace the transformer; if it does, have an electrician inspect the circuit.

3 When running the wires from the switches to the chimes, label which wire goes to the front of the house and which goes to the back. Then connect the front wire to the front chimes terminal, and the back-door switch wire to the rear terminal.

1 Begin by choosing a good location for the chimes unit, which usually means mounting it near the center of the house. Once the site is located, attach the chimes unit to the wall (top). Then mount a push-button switch at each entrance to the house.

2 Strip the wire insulation from the ends of all the wires that connect the push-button switches with the low-voltage transformer and chimes. Then attach one red wire from each switch to one of the terminal screws on the transformer.

4 Once the switch wires are attached to the transformer, run another wire from the second terminal on the transformer to the terminal marked trans on the chimes. Tighten it securely in place.

5 Install the chimes cover to the chimes base and test the installation.

STRAIGHT HOME-RUN WIRING SYSTEM

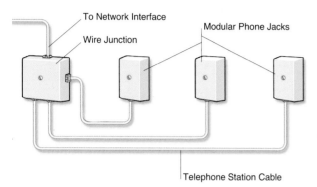

To Network Interface

Modular Phone Jacks

Wire Junction

Telephone Station Cable

OPEN-LOOP WIRING SYSTEM

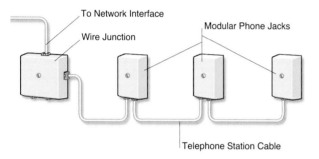

To Network Interface

Modular Phone Jacks

Wire Junction

Telephone Station Cable

CLOSED-LOOP WIRING SYSTEM

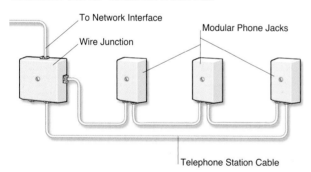

To Network Interface

Modular Phone Jacks

Wire Junction

Telephone Station Cable

Telephone wiring can be run using either a home-run system, in which each telephone jack is directly wired to a wire junction, or a loop system, in which wiring runs from jack to jack in an open or closed loop that returns to the wire junction and provides a second wiring path. Up to three jacks may be wired to one wire junction. A wire break to an independent jack will only cut service to the phone on that one line. A break in an open-loop system cuts service to any phones beyond the break. But a break in a closed-loop system won't stop a signal from traveling to the break point from either direction.

Wiring a Telephone Jack

As with most other wiring projects, the hardest part of the procedure is fishing the telephone cable to the location of the phone jack. This type of project has the added disadvantage of using very small wires, so working with them can become frustrating at times. Begin by running the cable from the junction box to the new jack. Strip the wires, and attach them to the color-coded terminals. Mount the jack on the wall, and you are finished.

1 Start installing a new phone jack by removing the cover to the wire junction box and stripping 2 in. of sheathing from the end of a D-station cable. Strip the insulation from the ends of the wires, and attach each colored wire to its matching-colored terminal.

Punch-Down Blocks

Newer phone systems, instead of screw-terminal junction blocks, use punch-down, or connection, blocks. They are also known as insulation displacement connectors (IDCs). A standard M, or 66, block has connections for 25 pairs of wires. Additional blocks can be added if needed. A special punch-down tool presses the telephone wires into a 66 block, eliminating the need to strip the wires before connecting them to the block.

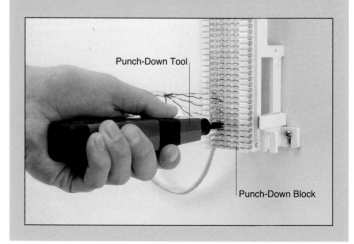

Punch-Down Tool

Punch-Down Block

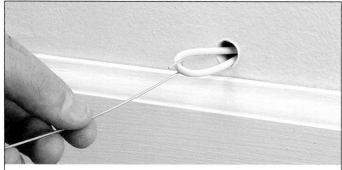

2 Choose a good location for the jack, and drill a hole through the drywall for cable access. Then fish the phone cable into this hole (top). Strip off about 2 in. of cable sheathing; then remove the insulation from the end of each wire.

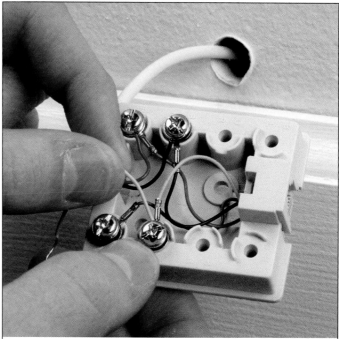

3 Bring the stripped cable into the bottom of the phone jack, and attach like-colored wires to the same terminals. Tighten the screws securely; mount the jack on the wall; and screw the jack cover to the jack.

4 Using a telephone line tester, test the polarity of the telephone jack wiring. A green light indicates correct wiring.

5 Plug a telephone cord into the jack, and listen for a dial tone. If you get one, make a call, and check that the line sounds clear.

6 Specialty Wiring

chapter 7

outdoor wiring

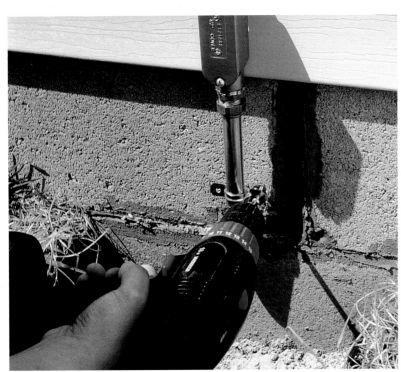

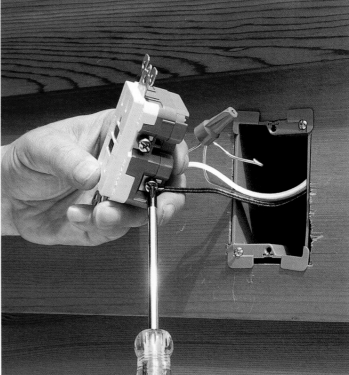

OUTDOOR POWER AND LIGHTING enables you to light walkways, driveways, pools, patios, and yards to maintain the safety and security of your home. You will need exterior receptacles to power outdoor appliances, tools, and equipment. Before providing this power and lighting, however, you must be aware of how it differs from interior power and lighting and be familiar with the different code requirements. Some communities require a licensed electrician to do outdoor wiring, while others simply demand that the work be inspected by one before you use it. The strictest localities require inspections by a licensed electrical inspector.

What Makes It Different
Circuiting

Underground or overhead outdoor wiring needs protection from the elements. It's subjected to wet and icy conditions, drastic changes in temperature, corrosion, frost heaves, yard tools, and excavation equipment. Overhead cable must be kept high enough not to pose a hazard to anyone or anything passing beneath it. Generally, a height of 12 feet is adequate for residential work, but does nothing to guard against falling tree limbs and swinging ladders. To avoid these risks, burying the cable is usually a better option.

Overhead Cable Requirements

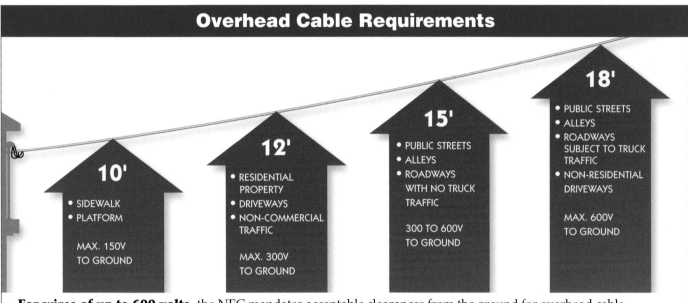

10'
• SIDEWALK
• PLATFORM

MAX. 150V TO GROUND

12'
• RESIDENTIAL PROPERTY
• DRIVEWAYS
• NON-COMMERCIAL TRAFFIC

MAX. 300V TO GROUND

15'
• PUBLIC STREETS
• ALLEYS
• ROADWAYS WITH NO TRUCK TRAFFIC

300 TO 600V TO GROUND

18'
• PUBLIC STREETS
• ALLEYS
• ROADWAYS SUBJECT TO TRUCK TRAFFIC
• NON-RESIDENTIAL DRIVEWAYS

MAX. 600V TO GROUND

For wires of up to 600 volts, the NEC mandates acceptable clearances from the ground for overhead cable spans (Section 225.18).

Outdoor Conduit and Cable

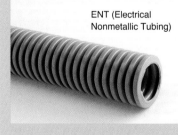

ENT (Electrical Nonmetallic Tubing)

Flexible nonmetallic conduit offers limited protection for underground cable or conductors.

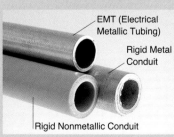

EMT (Electrical Metallic Tubing)

Rigid Metal Conduit

Rigid Nonmetallic Conduit

Rigid conduit affords extra protection for underground cable, but water penetration and eventual corrosion remain an inevitable problem.

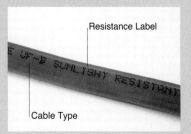

Resistance Label

Cable Type

Type UF (underground feeder) cable is designed for direct burial underground. The sheathing label indicates whether it is also sunlight and corrosion resistant.

Standard NM Cable

UF Cable

UF cable doesn't have paper insulation between the wires and outer sheathing. A thermoplastic coating encases the wires, making them water resistant but difficult to strip.

Trenching

Digging a trench without first knowing what is underneath can be extremely dangerous. If you excavate randomly, you may unwittingly cut into a sewer or water pipe, or a telephone, cable TV, or electrical power line. Before you do any digging, be sure to check with your local utility company and have it mark the location of any underground utility lines where you plan to dig. In most areas, you are required by law to inform your utility company and secure its approval before you do any excavating. Once you are cleared to excavate, you can dig your trench using a shovel, mattock, backhoe, trencher, or any other suitable equipment. Keep your trenches as short and narrow as possible to reduce expenses and keep landscaping damage to a minimum. Also, when you run UF cable in a trench, always be sure to leave a slack loop for expansion wherever the cable enters or leaves the pipe (conduit). The cable will respond to changes in temperature. Pulling the cable tight will result in damage or even a complete break because of the soil pressure against the cable.

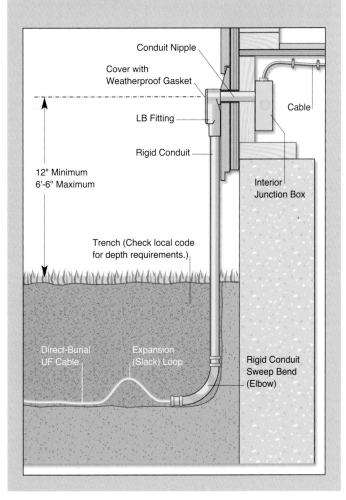

Conduit Nipple

Cover with
Weatherproof Gasket

Cable

LB Fitting

Rigid Conduit

12" Minimum
6'-6" Maximum

Interior
Junction Box

Trench (Check local code
for depth requirements.)

Direct-Burial
UF Cable

Expansion
(Slack) Loop

Rigid Conduit
Sweep Bend
(Elbow)

Installing UF Cable

UF cable is waterproof and specifically designed to be installed underground. The insulation that encapsulates the wires is very rugged. But it still needs some protection when it's exposed to possible damage. That's why the code calls for rigid conduit protection above grade and where the cable enters or leaves a building.

1 Lay out the path of your trench from the LB fitting on the house to the cable's destination point, using wooden stakes and mason's string.

4 Inside the junction box, attach the NM power cable from the service panel to the UF cable coming from the trench outside. Join the white wires, the black wires, and the ground wires (using a grounding pigtail) under separate wire connectors. Attach the free end of the pigtail to the grounding screw inside the box.

2 Dig the trench by hand, using a shovel, or rent a backhoe for the job. Set aside the sod so it can be put on top when the trench is refilled.

3 Attach a conduit sweep to the conduit coming out of the bottom of the LB fitting. Install a plastic bushing on the open end. Then feed the cable into the sweep, up through the conduit, into the LB fitting, through the house wall, and into the junction box.

5 Once the cables are attached in the junction box, continue laying the UF cable. Form an expansion loop in the cable next to the conduit sweep, and at any point where the cable enters or leaves rigid conduit, to prevent it from being stretched tight with changes in temperature.

6 When the cable installation is complete, carefully refill the trench with the soil that was excavated. When all the loose soil is back in place, cover it with the pieces of sod that were set aside earlier. Tamp them down using a tamping tool, garden rake, or the back of a shovel.

Outdoor Wiring Methods

Receptacles

Standard metal or plastic boxes are not acceptable outdoors because they aren't watertight. Watertight receptacle boxes are made of plastic, aluminum, bronze, or zinc-coated steel. If the cable is direct-burial type UF, it can be run directly in a trench at the code-specified depth. Wherever cable is exposed it must be protected in rigid conduit. Check your local code for variations.

PRO TIP

Trenching under Sidewalks

If underground (UF) cable must be run beneath a sidewalk or a driveway, then the cable must be protected in rigid conduit. Run the trench for your direct-burial cable right up to the sidewalk or driveway; then continue it on the opposite side. To bridge the gap between the two trenches, cut a length of rigid metal conduit approximately 12 inches longer than the width to be spanned. You have a couple of options. One way is to flatten the end of the pipe, and drive it beneath the slab using a sledgehammer. Another, preferred, way is to put a cap on the end of the pipe, and pound it through. If you crimped the end of the pipe, cut off the damaged section. If you used the cap method, remove the cap; then push the cable through the pipe.

Installing an Outdoor Receptacle

Outdoor receptacles must be protected with a GFCI. Like the inside of your house, you can provide this protection by installing a GFCI receptacle or a GFCI circuit breaker. Because these receptacles tend to trip periodically without cause, most people think it makes more sense to use the breakers. They may cost more, but they're less troublesome.

Wet-Rated Boxes

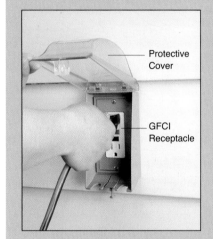

Protective Cover

GFCI Receptacle

For receptacles that are exposed to heavy weather and heavy use, choose one with a flip-up plastic cover that protects the box entirely while the plug is installed.

3 Strip the thermoplastic coating from the wires. This can be difficult to do. Start by cutting the plastic with a utility knife. Then pull the plastic off the ends of the wire using pliers. When all this coating is gone, strip the insulation off the individual wires.

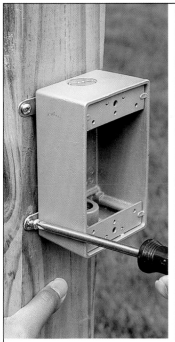

1 Begin by mounting an outdoor receptacle box on the side wall of a building, a porch, a deck, or a free-standing post. Screw the mounting ears securely to the surface (left). Or mount the receptacle on the top of some rigid metal conduit that is anchored in concrete (right).

2 Once the receptacle is mounted, install a plastic bushing in the end of the conduit to prevent the cable from chafing against any sharp edges. Then pull the cable up through the conduit so about 8 in. extends into the box.

4 Attach the black wire to the brass screw terminal and the white wire to the silver screw terminal. Attach the grounding wire to the grounding screw on the side of the receptacle.

5 Push the wires inside the box; then screw the receptacle in place. Seal the perimeter of the receptacle with the foam gasket that came with box. Keep the gasket aligned as you install the box cover so that it doesn't become distorted and possibly leak as a result.

Installing a Motion-Sensor Light

Lights

Employ exterior lighting to provide required illumination and task lighting, or go further by providing decorative and accent lighting. Combined with motion sensors, you can even use exterior lighting as a part of your home security system. All outdoor lighting, whether practical or decorative, must be weatherproof. You can mount an exterior light on a porch ceiling, building wall, or free-standing post. Pipe-mounted fixtures are secured by a threaded compression fitting, while floodlights require special lamp-socket fittings having movable heads that can be adjusted in any direction. An additional movable head is often furnished for attaching a motion sensor. Infrared motion detectors trip on the lights whenever an object passes within a given field of vision. A photocell prevents the device from tripping during daylight hours, and a timing mechanism determines the length of light operation in the absence of continued motion. You can use a manually operated indoor switch to override the automatic control. You can also control your floodlights using an indoor timer-switch in place of a conventional manual switch.

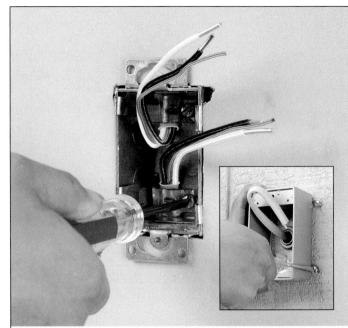

1 To install an outdoor light fixture that has a built-in motion sensor, first install a switch box on the inside of the house. Fish a power cable and a cable from the light fixture into this box. Then mount an outdoor box on the exterior wall, and fish the cable from the switch into this box (inset).

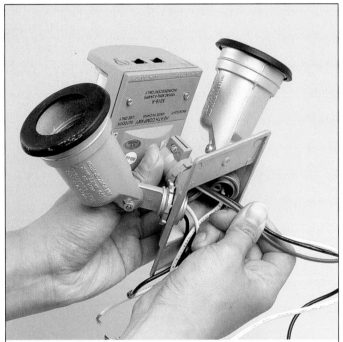

3 Assemble the light fixture according to the manufacturer's directions. Usually, the two light sockets and the single motion-detector unit are held to the fixture base with retaining nuts tightened from inside using pliers. Untangle all the lead wires.

4 Slide a foam gasket over the fixture wires and against the base of the fixture. Then join all the white wires with a wire connector and all the ground wires with another wire connector. Join the hot leads from the box, the two lights, and the sensor unit according to the manufacturer's directions.

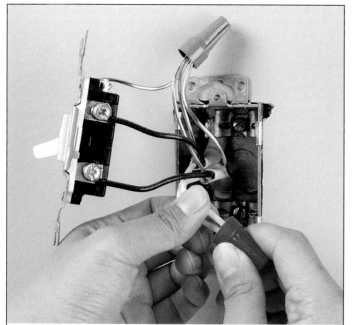

2 Attach the two black (hot) wires to the switch terminals, and join the two white (neutral) wires with a wire connector. Use another connector to join the ground wires to a pigtail. Then attach the free end of the pigtail to the grounding screw in the fixture box, if it's metal, or to the ground screw on the switch.

5 Carefully tuck the wires into the box, and press the fixture into place. Make sure the gasket remains properly aligned to ensure a weatherproof fit. Then screw the fixture to the box. Install the bulbs; turn on the power; and test for proper operation.

Outdoor Receptacle, Switch, and Fixture Circuit

A GFCI receptacle protects the circuit wires as well as the switch and fixture from shock damage in this outdoor circuit. Two-wire cable feeds power to the line screw terminal on the receptacle and proceeds to the switch and fixture from the load terminal.

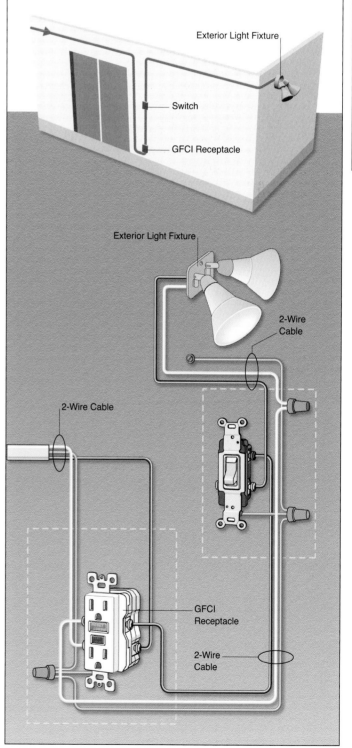

Installing Low-Voltage Lighting

Low-Voltage Lighting

The most popular type of outdoor lighting is low-voltage lighting. Because of the low voltage needed to power this type of lighting, it is much safer to use outdoors than lighting powered by a conventional 120-volt line. It is so low, in fact, that a short-circuit in low-voltage underwater lighting would not even be felt by a swimmer. For this reason, it is the ideal type of lighting for inground pools. More often, though, low-voltage lighting is employed to light a drive or pathway or to accent landscaping. Lamps for low-voltage lighting commonly range between 25 to 50 watts. To get these lower voltages, you install a transformer to step down standard 120-volt service. Lighting controlled from a transformer can be strung together and connected to fixtures that can then be spiked into the ground along the length of the low-voltage wiring. Because there is little hazard associated with this kind of wiring, it doesn't need to be buried any deeper than 6 inches. When assembling the components, determine the length of the wiring runs, which will tell you what size wiring to buy. (The manufacturer can help determine wiring size.) Unlike typical line-voltage lights, low-voltage lights can have a drop off in power the farther away from the house they are located. Using a heavier wire gauge prevents this.

1 Determine a good location for an outdoor receptacle; then trace the perimeter of a box on the siding, and drill saw-blade access holes in the corners. Cut out the waste using a saber saw or a reciprocating saw. Then fish a power cable into the box, and attach the box to the wall.

Small pools of light cast by these path fixtures light the way and provide a decorative accent to the yard.

4 Once the light heads are positioned in the soil, dig a 6-in.-deep trench between the lights, and lay the low-voltage cable in the bottom of the trench. Join the leads from the light heads to the cable using their self-piercing clips.

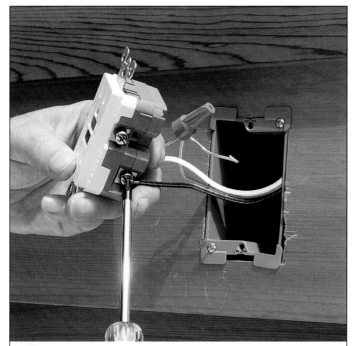

2 Attach the black (hot) and white (neutral) wires to the terminals on a GFCI receptacle. Then join the bare ground wire to a grounding pigtail that attaches either to the ground screw on the receptacle or a grounding screw in a metal box.

3 Position the light heads along the walkway, driveway, or other feature that you want to illuminate. Follow the manufacturer's recommendations to get the best light coverage from the units.

5 Connect the underground power cables to the back of the transformer, following the manufacturer's instructions. Usually all that's required to make a good connection is to slide the cable wires under self-piercing terminal screws and to tighten the screws.

6 Mount the transformer on the wall next to the GFCI receptacle. Then plug the power pigtail cord from the transformer into the receptacle. Close the weatherproof cover; turn on the power to the circuit; and check for proper operation.

glossary

AC Alternating current. The type of current found in most home electrical systems in the United States.

AWG American Wire Gauge, a system of sizing wire.

Ampere, amperage, amps A unit of measurement that describes the rate of electrical flow. Amperes are measured in terms of the number of electrons flowing through a given point in a conductor in one second. Conductors are rated by their *ampacity*, the current in amperes they can carry continuously under conditions of use without exceeding their temperature ratings.

Arc-fault circuit interrupter A safety circuit breaker that detects an arcing situation in a circuit, such as a loose connection or damaged wiring.

BX cable Electrical cable wrapped in a protective, flexible, metal sheathing. BX contains at least two conductors. Some codes limit its use. Seldom used.

Ballast Device that controls the current in a fluorescent light.

Black wire In a cable, the wire that normally functions as a hot wire.

CO/ALR Marking that designates switches and receptacles that may be used with aluminum wiring.

CSA Canadian Standards Association. *See* National Electrical Code.

CU/AL Marking that designates receptacles and switches that may be used with copper or copper-clad aluminum wire.

Cable Two or more wires grouped together inside a protective sheathing of plastic or metal.

Cartridge fuse Cylindrical fuses that are rated to carry higher voltages and current levels than plug fuses. Two types: with and without blade contacts.

Circuit breaker A protective device that opens a circuit automatically when a given overcurrent occurs. Can also be operated and reset manually.

Common The identified terminal on a three-way switch. Usually has a dark-color screw; may be marked COM.

Conduit Metal or plastic tubing designed to enclose electrical wires.

Continuity tester A device that indicates when a complete electrical patch exists between two points.

DC Direct current. The electrical current supplied by a battery and often an engine-driven generator.

Double-pole switch A switch with four terminals that controls a single major appliance. The toggle is marked ON/OFF.

End-of-the-run Box with its outlet or switch at the final position in a circuit.

Energy efficiency rating (EER) The relative amount of energy consumed by a given appliance. The higher the EER, the more efficient it is.

Fuse A safety device designed to protect house circuits. A metal wire inside the fuse melts or disintegrates in case of overload or short circuit, thus shutting off the current. *See also* Cartridge fuse.

Green wire In a cable, the wire that functions as an equipment grounding conductor.

Ground-fault circuit interrupter (GFCI) A safety circuit breaker that compares the amount of current entering a receptacle on the hot wire with the amount leaving on the white wire. If there is a discrepancy of 0.005 amperes, the GFCI breaks the circuit in $\frac{1}{40}$ of a second. Required by code in areas that are subject to dampness.

Grounding electrode conductor (Ground wire) Wire that carries current to earth in the event of a short circuit. The ground wire is essential to the safety of your house wiring system and of its users.

Incoming wire Hot wire that feeds power into a box.

Jumper wires Short lengths of single wire used to complete circuit connections.

Junction box Metal or plastic box inside which all standard wire splices and wiring connections must be made.

Kilowatt (kW) 1,000 watts.

Middle-of-the-run Box with its outlets or switch lying between the power source and another box. Cable(s) enters and leaves this box.

NM cable Cable for use in dry locations.

NMC cable Cable used in damp and dry locations, but not in wet locations.

National Electrical Code Body of regulations spelling out minimum safe, functional electrical procedures. Local codes add to NEC regulations.

Overload Too great a demand for power made on a circuit.

Pigtail A short piece of wire used to complete a circuit inside a box.

Polarized plug Plug with no ground. One blade is wider than the other.

Recoded wire White-insulated wire that has been taped or painted black. The recoding indicates that the wire now carries power.

Red wire In a cable, the wire designated as a hot wire. Usually used as a traveler in three-way switches.

Romex Plastic-sheathed NM cable containing at least two conductors.

Service panel The point at which electricity provided by a local utility enters your house wiring system.

Short circuit A fault that occurs when a hot or ungrounded wire touches a grounded (white) or grounding (bare or green) wire or a grounded object.

Starter A switch in a fluorescent light that closes the circuit only when sufficient power is available.

Switch loop Installation in which a fixture is installed between a power source and a switch. The power passes through the fixture box to the switch. The switch then sends power to the fixture itself.

TW wire Type of wire most often used in home circuits and exterior conduit.

Three-way switch One of two switches controlling a single outlet or fixture; it has three terminals. The toggle is not marked ON/OFF.

Traveler wire Transfers electricity from one three-way switch to another.

UF cable Cable for use in wet outdoor and underground locations; also used in buildings in areas exposed to wetness.

Underwriters Laboratories (UL) Independent organization that tests electrical products for safe operation and conformance with published standards under various conditions. Products that pass may display the UL logo.

Volt, voltage Unit of measurement of the electromotive force of a current. Volts multiplied by amps give the wattage available in a circuit (V x A = W).

Watt, wattage Unit of measurement of the amount of electrical power required or consumed by a fixture or appliance. See also Ampere and Volt.

White wire White-insulated wire that forms a circuit with a power wire.

Wire connector Plastic cap-like device used to splice wires. The inside is threaded metal, which grips the wires.

Zip cord Line cord designed with a thin section between the insulating coverings of the wires. The cord easily splits when pulled down the middle.

index

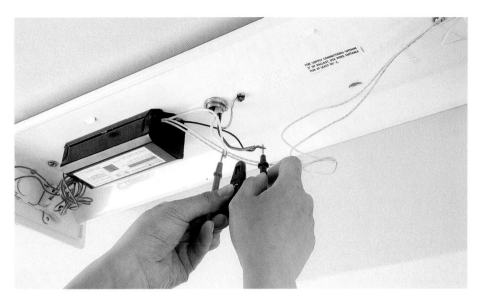

Metric Conversion

Length

1 inch	25.4 mm
1 foot	0.3048 m
1 yard	0.9144 m
1 mile	1.61 km

Area

1 square inch	645 mm^2
1 square foot	0.0929 m^2
1 square yard	0.8361 m^2
1 acre	4046.86 m^2
1 square mile	2.59 km^2

Volume

1 cubic inch	16.3870 cm^3
1 cubic foot	0.03 m^3
1 cubic yard	0.77 m^3

Common Lumber Equivalents

Sizes: Metric cross sections are so close to their U.S. sizes, as noted below, that for most purposes they may be considered equivalents.

Dimensional	1 x 2	19 x 38 mm
lumber	1 x 4	19 x 89 mm
	2 x 2	38 x 38 mm
	2 x 4	38 x 89 mm
	2 x 6	38 x 140 mm
	2 x 8	38 x 184 mm
	2 x 10	38 x 235 mm
	2 x 12	38 x 286 mm
Sheet	4 x 8 ft.	1200 x 2400 mm
sizes	4 x 10 ft.	1200 x 3000 mm
Sheet	¼ in.	6 mm
thicknesses	⅜ in.	9 mm
	½ in.	12 mm
	¾ in.	19 mm
Stud/joist	16 in. o.c.	400 mm o.c.
spacing	24 in. o.c.	600 mm o.c.

Capacity

1 fluid ounce	29.57 mL
1 pint	473.18 mL
1 quart	1.14 L
1 gallon	3.79 L

Weight

1 ounce	28.35g
1 pound	0.45kg

Temperature

Celsius = Fahrenheit – 32 x ⅝
Fahrenheit = Celsius x 1.8 + 32